THROUGH THE EYES
OF A CHILD

Your Ultimate Guide to Parenting Your Inner Child

Linda and Michael Brady

Partners for Karmic Freedom Inc.

Copyright 2021 by Partners for Karmic Freedom, Inc.
All rights reserved. No part of this book may be reproduced or transmitted in any form or by any means, electronic or mechanical, including photocopying, recording, or any information storage and retrieval system without permission in writing from the authors.

Published by Partners for Karmic Freedom, Inc. 2021
Printed in the United States of America
Book Design by Matthew Brady
Cover Design by Tarin Pratte, Memphremagog Press
ISBN 978-0-9748399-2-9

First Edition

FOREWORD

I have known Linda Brady for over 12 years. She has been my coach, teacher, colleague, collaborator, and friend. We have shared clients, supporting them through deep transformational work. Linda awakened my inner mother and inner child, healing the wound that wanted to destroy my vitality. This awakening developed an embodied integrated relationship with my soul. I have used her teachings to support hundreds of clients in finding their own inner child. I have called this the act of "re-mothering" yourself as a way to welcome home your inner child.

As a psychotherapist and life coach, I learned the tools of internal family systems, which encourage us to grasp our internal roles or parts of self. In a therapeutic setting, we invite the curiosity of a client to explore the inner social world of the self or ego. Big awakenings happen for those who emotionally connect with the most vulnerable parts of the self. This has greater impact when we create time and space for concretizing these roles or characters from our inner world. Reading this book to gain information will leave you with just that…information. Choosing to do the "work" in an embodied, emotional way creates a living breathing experience…and THAT has the capacity to change lives.

Linda Brady has expertly designed an invitation for such a journey. She welcomes the reader to participate in the experience of "inner storytelling." When we work with such themes as our inner child or the memory of our childhood self through tangible means, we can meet these personality patterns with less fear as they become more approachable and thus knowable. As Toko-Pa Turner said in the book Belonging: Remembering Ourselves Home, "In order to heal the scarcity wound created by the lack of nurturing both in families and in our culture, we must learn to become the loving mother to ourselves that we never had."

I invite you to take the action Linda has outlined here. Don't read **Through the Eyes of a Child: The Ultimate Guide to Parenting Your Inner Child** and put it down! That wastes your time. That dishonors your inner soul and creates more internal unconscious separation. Instead, dive in, take the leap, and do the work! Show up! Be accountable to yourself. Take the risk to be vulnerable and see if your "authentic self" has the courage to find, greet, nurture, and connect with your inner child. This may be the most sacred act you ever choose to do. Are you willing to show up? Are you willing to be kind? Are you willing to take action? Do you want to live an integrated life? If so, then create a sacred space, close your eyes, and welcome your inner child to the playroom of your heart. Then, open up those eyes and walk forward in life as the integrated soul that you are meant to become; free, mature, truthful, whole, and complete.

**Katharine P. Knapp, LPC, SEP,
Director of Creative Integration Therapy**

ACKNOWLEDGMENTS

Michael and I thank all of our clients and students for their experiences and for taking the time to write them for this book. We could not have written it without you. We thank all of our friends, who are our extended Aquarian family, for encouraging us to complete this book. "It is about time," many said. Last, we personally thank our inner children, Lynnie and Mikey. They are the joy of our lives now. Their laugh, brightness, devotion to God, and their deep desire to help people have provided us insight, love, and spiritual energy to continue our work.

Linda and Michael Brady

A SPECIAL GIFT

You will need your astrological chart to get the most from our book. We are happy to provide that for you at a nominal cost. Please e-mail your date, time, and place of birth to karmic freedom @gmail.com. We will e-mail you a packet containing your astrological chart, a card that describes your soul mission, and a table to aid you in translating your astrological symbols into English. Michael and I wish you and your inner child a blessed journey filled with love, fun, happiness, and growth.

Linda and Michael Brady
Partners for Karmic Freedom, Inc.

MEDITATIONS

Michael Brady has provided five powerful meditations to augment your inner child experience. Links are provided to refer you to the meditation on our website, KarmicFreedom.com. You are free to purchase all five or select one or more. Please refer to our shopping cart for more information.

TESTIMONIALS

I met Linda and Michael Brady in 2006, when my inner child decided to launch herself into the unknown. She and I had just read "Discover Your Soul Mission" and then decided to go to a small town in Jay, Vermont. We wanted to stay with these two wonderful souls that my soul had known for so many lives. Thanks to my Moon in Sagittarius, my inner child loves to throw herself into new lands in search of universal wisdom. It was with this joy and enthusiasm that I went to the "blind meeting" with Linda and Michael. For 15 years, we have been partners on a wonderful journey that has spanned this and other lives. They have taught me so much about how to manifest my soul mission as a professional astrologer. I am eternally grateful for this wonderful karmic blessing.

—**Priscila Lima de Charbonnieres, founder of Soulloop**

Forming a relationship with my inner child has been one of the most important endeavors of my life. Linda's unique use of astrology has helped me uncover the issues of my wounded inner child layer by layer. Working with her has made all the difference in the world in my journey toward healing.

—**Richard Hoshal, broadcast journalist**

I have had the honor of learning and practicing karmic astrology with Linda Brady for close to 20 years. While I thought I understood the notion of my inner child, Linda offers an entirely more exciting and interesting way of healing, understanding, and nurturing her. When I ignore my child, she stirs up chaos in my life. When I heal my karmic issues with her, I find the tools to create the life I have always wanted to have. Linda's work healing that child is a can't-miss!

—**Sue Ouellette, CRNP, PMHNP, CSP, nurse practitioner**

Working with the Bradys has enlightened me as to my emotional connection with my inner child. I have come to realize that when I feel happy, my inner child is content and satisfied. When I am sad, my inner child is likely feeling neglected, and when I am frustrated or even angry, it is my abused inner child that has simply had enough! This awareness has given me so much more control over my life.

—**Debra Chadick, real estate appraiser**

Table of Contents

Section 1	NOTES FROM THE AUTHORS	1
Section 2	INNER CHILD ASSESSMENT	3
Section 3	OUR PHILOSOPHY	5

Understanding Child Abuse 10
Meeting My Childhood "Friends" 15

Section 4	I BECOME AN ASTROLOGER	32
Section 5	DISCOVERING MY INNER CHILD	36

Lynnie Becomes Real 38
Finding the Safe Place 43
Anne's Experience 45

Section 6	CHILDHOOD EMOTIONAL DECLARATIONS	49

Mark's Story 51
Your Early Declarations and Their Impact 54

Section 7	COMMUNICATION: THE KEY TO UNDERSTANDING YOUR INNER CHILD	56

The Four Filters and Their Elements 59
   Mercury in Earth: Taurus, Virgo, and Capricorn 61
   Mercury in Water: Cancer, Scorpio, and Pisces 62
   Mercury in Air: Gemini, Libra, and Aquarius 63
   Mercury in Fire: Aries, Leo, and Sagittarius 64

The Four Filters at Work in the Classroom	65
Your Inner Child's Mercury	71
Mercury in Aries	71
Mercury in Taurus	74
Mercury in Gemini	76
Mercury in Cancer	78
Mercury in Leo	80
Mercury in Virgo	82
Mercury in Libra	85
Mercury in Scorpio	88
Mercury in Sagittarius	91
Mercury in Capricorn	94
Mercury in Aquarius	97
Mercury in Pisces	100
Section 8 YOUR EMOTIONAL INNER CHILD	**103**
The Value of Emotions	105
The Astrological Moon	106
For My Male Readers	113
Moon in Aries	115
Comforting Relationship with Mother	117
Challenging Relationship with Mother	117
Moon in Taurus	120
Comforting Relationship with Mother	121
Challenging Relationship with Mother	122
Moon in Gemini	124
Comforting Relationship with Mother	126
Challenging Relationship with Mother	126
Moon in Cancer	128
Comforting Relationship with Mother	130
Challenging Relationship with Mother	130
Moon in Leo	132
Comforting Relationship with Mother	133

Challenging Relationship with Mother	134
Moon in Virgo	136
Comforting Relationship with Mother	138
Challenging Relationship with Mother	138
Moon in Libra	141
Comforting Relationship with Mother	142
Challenging Relationship with Mother	143
Moon in Scorpio	145
Comforting Relationship with Mother	146
Challenging Relationship with Mother	147
Moon in Sagittarius	149
Comforting Relationship with Mother	150
Challenging Relationship with Mother	151
Moon in Capricorn	153
Comforting Relationship with Mother	154
Challenging Relationship with Mother	155
Moon in Aquarius	157
Comforting Relationship with Mother	158
Challenging Relationship with Mother	159
Moon in Pisces	161
Comforting Relationship with Mother	162
Challenging Relationship with Mother	163
Inner Moon Worksheet	164
Michael's Story	169
Michael's Story, Part 2: My Inner Child "Mikey"	178
Section 9 SATURN AND YOUR INNER FATHER	**186**
Your Saturn	186
For My Female Readers	187
Saturn in Aries	190
Comforting Relationship with Mother	191
Challenging Relationship with Mother	192

Saturn in Taurus	193
Comforting Relationship with Mother	194
Challenging Relationship with Mother	195
Saturn in Gemini	196
Comforting Relationship with Mother	197
Challenging Relationship with Mother	198
Saturn in Cancer	200
Comforting Relationship with Mother	201
Challenging Relationship with Mother	202
Saturn in Leo	203
Comforting Relationship with Mother	204
Challenging Relationship with Mother	204
Saturn in Virgo	206
Comforting Relationship with Mother	207
Challenging Relationship with Mother	208
Saturn in Libra	209
Comforting Relationship with Mother	210
Challenging Relationship with Mother	210
Saturn in Scorpio	212
Comforting Relationship with Mother	213
Challenging Relationship with Mother	214
Saturn in Sagittarius	215
Comforting Relationship with Mother	216
Challenging Relationship with Mother	216
Saturn in Capricorn	218
Comforting Relationship with Mother	219
Challenging Relationship with Mother	220
Saturn in Aquarius	221
Comforting Relationship with Mother	222
Challenging Relationship with Mother	222
Saturn in Pisces	224
Comforting Relationship with Mother	225
Challenging Relationship with Mother	226
Inner Father Worksheet	227
Challenges to Discovering Your Inner Child	230

Karen's Challenges	230

Section 10 STRATEGIES TO HELP YOU DISCOVER YOUR INNER CHILD — 233

Find Early Childhood Pictures	237
Meditation	239
Find Your Baby Book	240
Listen to Your Family's Stories	241
Observe Other Children	242
Draw a Picture of Your Inner Child	243

Section 11 PARENTING TIPS — 245

The Moon and Your Inner Mother	245
Moon and Aries	247
Moon and Taurus	249
Moon and Gemini	251
Moon and Cancer	253
Moon and Leo	255
Moon and Virgo	257
Moon and Libra	259
Moon and Scorpio	261
Moon and Sagittarius	263
Moon and Capricorn	265
Moon and Aquarius	267
Moon and Pisces	269
Saturn and Your Inner Father	271
Saturn and Aries	273
Saturn and Taurus	275
Saturn and Gemini	277
Saturn and Cancer	279
Saturn and Leo	281
Saturn and Virgo	283
Saturn and Libra	285

Saturn and Scorpio	287
Saturn and Sagittarius	289
Saturn and Capricorn	291
Saturn and Aquarius	293
Saturn and Pisces	295
Meditation: Divine Mother and Father	297
Inner Divine Mother Notes	298
Inner Divine Father Notes	299
Inner Parents Worksheet	300
Your Commitment Letter	303

Section 12   THE SANCTUARY   306

Creating the Sanctuary	306
Sanctuary Meditation	309
Sanctuary Meditation Notes	310

Section 13   YOUR INNER JOYFUL CHILD   311

Your Favorite Childhood Activities	315
Meditation: Your Inner Joyful Child	318
Draw a Picture of the Joyful Child	319

Section 14   YOUR INNER CHILD AND DREAMING   321

The Value of Dreaming	321
If You Have Trouble Remembering Your Dreams	327
	331
Two Dream Examples and Interpretations	332
Techniques for Better Dreaming	334
Meditation for Better Sleep and Dreaming	335

Section 15   YOUR INNER CHILD AND YOUR ADULT RELATIONSHIPS   337

Section 16	YOUR KARMIC CHILD	340
Section 17	CONCLUSION: BECOMING THE SPIRITUAL ADULT	346
Section 18	ADDENDUM	349

Astrological Symbolism 350
Sample Dream Journal 362

NOTES FROM THE AUTHORS

Michael and I are holistic astrologers who believe in becoming spiritual adults as we navigate the new age of Aquarius we are now entering. We also believe that our astrological charts have priceless information to accomplish this goal. Even though this book is dedicated to the importance of embracing, knowing, and honoring the child who lives within you, it still carries within it vital information in how to guide your biological children. Having your astrological chart is critical in aiding you embrace and support your inner and outer children. Because of this, we are offering your astrological chart free as the companion to this book.

Through the Eyes of a Child: The Ultimate Guide in Parenting Your Inner Child incorporates 60 years of our combined astrological experience in aiding clients as they embrace and support their inner child and their family. This is the guidebook that clients have requested.

My husband, Michael, has shared my vision for a guidebook for the inner child for years. His gentle, loving meditations bring the book to life. I challenge each one of you, my dear readers, to take my 1-month challenge. Enjoy the presence of your precious little one, have more fun, and be happy! You have chosen this guidebook for a reason. Maybe I have suggested it. Maybe a friend gave it to you as a gift. Maybe you "accidently" found it on Amazon. For whatever reason, your soul has provided you an opportunity to find the wholeness and happiness you deserve. I believe that embracing your inner child will bring you this and much more. It will bring you peace. I invite you to take a month of your life to discover your inner child. Do the readings, analyze your astrological symbology, relax in the meditations, complete the exercises, and practice the strategies that I have created for you. Take a leap of faith to find your most precious part—your inner child.

INNER CHILD ASSESSMENT

- Have you claimed the little child within you?

    Yes   No

- If so, do you have a daily relationship with your inner child?   Yes   No

- Do you know how to physically nurture your inner child?

    Yes   No

- Do you love physical movement and exercise?

    Yes   No

- Have you created opportunities for childlike creativity?

    Yes   No

- Are you able to label, embrace, and express your emotions?   Yes   No

- Are you in touch with your unconscious behaviors that feel childlike?   Yes   No

- Do you remember dreams of children?

    Yes   No

❖ Do you know how to play?

                                         Yes   No

❖ Are you in connection with your inner mother?

                                           Yes   No

❖ Are you in connection with your inner father?

                                           Yes   No

❖ Do you experience spontaneity and joyful wonder?

                                           Yes   No

If you answered NO to most of these questions, our inner child guidebook will definitely help you find and embrace your inner child. Michael has provided five powerful meditations to connect you to the unconscious places where your inner child lives. In this guidebook, I have shared my personal journey in finding and parenting my inner child, Lynnie. It is filled with strategies, tools, and astrological insights. It will teach you how to listen to, protect, and nurture your inner child. I hope that you will enjoy this exciting journey in claiming this wonderful, precious part of yourself—your inner child.

OUR PHILOSOPHY

"We do not do what we want and yet we are responsible for what we are—that is the fact."

—**Jean-Paul Sartre**

I believe that, on an unconscious level, your personality links you to the seminal belief system that you learned from your parents; the hidden child within you; memories and pain that were not dealt with in your conscious life; and your night dreams, fears, and phobias. At this deep level, it also remembers personalities you've had from other lives and important information about who and what you have been. These memories of the thoughts, actions, and feelings of previous personalities share a common thread with you now, and they become the source of much of your unconscious motivation, impulse, angst, and relationship challenges. Your soul, in its infinite wisdom, has chosen your mother and father to provide you with very significant karmic information.

I always admired my mother for her compassion, her deep desire to serve humanity, her charm and graciousness, her love of books, and her writing skills. She was a dedicated woman who worked her way up the career ladder. Having had a major influence on the evolution of volunteerism in this country, my mother was an inspiration for me. She was open-minded and totally supported my need to leave the traditional world of education and become the holistic, astrological teacher and coach that I am today. Still, as a young girl, I became frustrated when my mother was committed to her work responsibilities at my expense. I felt abandoned and scared. It upset me that she could so easily sacrifice herself and her role as my mother for her career.

As I got older, I saw that I was doing the same thing. I was 46 years old and a workaholic. I sacrificed myself for my work. I had chosen my mother to show me myself. That was our karmic contract. Karma is complete only when we have balanced our previous actions through consciousness, commitment, and new actions. Our soul knows these situations and relationships and will create opportunities for us to resolve them. Our astrological chart, created by our soul, provides us with information about these karmic experiences as a spiritual reminder and a road map to navigating and understanding life's experiences. Many of us would agree that life doesn't seem fair. In my case, it was the sheer randomness of the world's inequities that moved me to study reincarnation as a viable possibility.

I had a notion of God as being fair and just, like a loving, wise father. I believed in a perfect universal order and a benign God. As a logical person, though, I couldn't understand why God would allow so many people to be subjected to such rampant tragedy and misery. It didn't make sense to me that this loving Father would give His children only one chance to learn and to right their lives. Providing them with many chances, many opportunities, made more sense to me. This conclusion helped me come to terms with the theory that there is a uniform fairness and justice in all our experiences, whether we perceive them as good or bad. We have many lives in which to practice, many lives in which to rebalance, many lives in which to become more God-like. Those who dismiss soul creation and discount the possibility of reincarnation often exhibit an either/or mentality. Some believe in heaven or hell as the ultimate reward or punishment. Others believe that fulfilling certain honorable duties in life affords one a higher standing in death. Fairness, to followers of this mutually exclusive philosophy, is measured by the barometer of how much good fortune comes to those who do good things. When bad things happen to good people, these people often become disillusioned. Their beliefs are broadsided, and they become confused, jaded, and angry. Many others adopt a fatalistic approach: They take life as it comes, believing that you live, you die, and that's it. They may not even entertain the abstract concepts of justice; they are too busy surviving their daily adversities.

I know that when I was a young adult, struggling to get through school and pay my bills, I had no time or energy to be philosophical about the meaning of life and to deal with the more abstract theories of justice. I met life every day on a pedestrian level, because it was what I had been taught to do. Many of the people I see are angry at God for allowing "bad things to happen." I had needed time to gain wisdom and maturity. I easily grasped the concept of self-creation because I had already seen evidence of the relationship between past crises and opportunities for self-awareness. However, taking responsibility for creating my whole life was a larger leap, one that proved very cathartic. Trusting the wisdom of my soul allowed me to release old anger, blame, and regret.

I treasured the journey and surrendered the results. Many clients come to me grieving the loss of a loved one. They tell me heart-wrenching stories involving the tragic death of a child, father, mother, brother or sister, or friend. My goal is to help them acknowledge that taking responsibility requires work—a discouraging prospect. We work at our jobs, we work on our relationships, we work on our physical health, we devote time to our children, and on and on. Now I'm proposing that you do even more: that you take a leap of faith and commit to being responsible for your actions, reactions, and life experience with your inner child.

Understanding Child Abuse

Many years ago, I felt inundated with very troubling stories and issues of child abuse. The news was filled with horrible stories of sexual, physical, and emotional abuse perpetrated on young children. I became obsessed with trying to figure out why it had become so prevalent. Why was it happening so much and becoming so public? Then, challenges with the Catholic Church and the priests who abused children were made known, and that really upset me. My husband and I began attracting adult clients with sexual, emotional, and physical abuse stemming from their childhoods. They were living their nightmares every day. I was beginning to understand more fully the imprints of childhood traumas not only as memories but also as realities concretized in their unconscious minds. Such reality was taking shape into a version of what I would later call the inner child

I believe that my soul and I create all situations in my life as an opportunity to learn. I began reflecting on what I was supposed to learn and why the issue of child abuse was haunting me. Was I an abused child? Or had I abused a child in other lives? I had never considered myself abused. I had actually believed that I had had a happy childhood; that is, until I began sharing my young life with my husband, Michael. He was appalled at some of my stories and was convinced that I had, in fact, been physically and emotionally abused. I had been sexually molested by a mentally disabled boy who was doing yard work at our house. The young man got caught, and I felt very guilty that he was going to get into trouble because of me. I had complete sympathy for him, and I took responsibility for the occurrence. When the police came to pick him up, I told them not to punish the young man, because I was smarter than he was. I was sacrificing myself to try to help somebody else, even at age 3, which is something I would continue to do throughout my life.

Strangely, in hindsight, that experience never felt like abuse to me. Somehow, it felt "meant to be" and inevitable. I later came to know that it was karmically equalizing. I was certain that I had disregarded and possibly abused children in other lives. The thought of taking care of children terrified me. I had chosen at age 30 not to have children. I was afraid that I would not know how to be a good parent. These were good reasons to be upset about child abuse, yet I knew that all of this was the tip of a very large iceberg. I took some deep breaths and began my journey to finding myself. I was a smart woman, always using my intelligence to get by. I have an undergraduate degree in psychology and a graduate degree in education, and I became a karmic astrologer when I was 39. I considered myself to be a philosopher.

I dismissed my emotions as being irrelevant and frivolous. I was a chubby child and became an obese woman, weighing in at 267 pounds. I disregarded my physical body and punished it by eating badly and smoking. I was totally out of touch with my unconscious mind and its emotional experiences. I had always been intellectually interested in Carl Jung's work. One day, I read—and I am paraphrasing—"the more you repressed your thoughts and feelings, the more you create external chaos and disease." I read and reread this line, hoping I could find a way to dismiss it. It described my life, and I was sick about it. It went against everything that had kept me strong and productive. I was not interested in opening up the Pandora's box that was my unconscious mind.

Then, to make matters worse, I read David

Spangler's book, Revelation. He wrote about seven laws of creating positive energy in your life. One that hit me between the eyes was the law of reversed effect. Simply stated, he opined that feelings trump intellect. He wrote that no matter how much you may want, on an intellectual level, to accomplish something, if your feelings run counter to your conscious wishes, you will not succeed. Terrific! I was in an existential crisis. All of my cherished beliefs were being challenged. I was still extremely overweight and unable to lose weight. I had quit smoking, which was hard but manageable. I could not conquer my addiction to carbs and sugar! I was becoming concerned about my physical health.

The incongruent thing was that I, as an astrologer, understood the parts of me that were symbolic of my emotional body. My astrological chart taught me the power of my soul and its purpose. I knew that my mission was to be courageous and open-hearted. I also knew that my soul would help me accomplish that. I honored that relationship with all of my heart—yet I was stubbornly not taking advantage of any of my astrological knowledge. Furthermore, I was actively turning my back on information given to me by two philosophers whom I respected: Carl Jung and David Spangler.

Meeting My Childhood "Friends"

The "whys" of my resistance became apparent when Michael and I went to see the movie "E.T. the Extra-Terrestrial," the charming tale of an adorable alien gardener stranded on Earth and befriended by three children. He falls ill, and soon his presence becomes known by the government. The children need to find a way for E.T. to go home and avoid government intervention. Throughout the movie and for weeks afterward, I was absolutely grief stricken, crying without any provocation, and emotionally obsessed with the E.T. character. I was as sad as I'd ever been in my entire life. We saw the movie again, thinking that

I would be less emotionally reactive. That didn't help. I would see E.T. figurines in stores and begin crying. I was inconsolable.

    Michael told me that how much I was crying and for how long did not make sense. It could not be just about the movie. He asked if it reminded me of anything in my childhood: "Did you lose anyone you loved when you were growing up? Was there a separation that caused you that kind of emotional pain?" I thought about his questions for several days and finally told him no. There was nothing that I could remember. I did not really know my father. He was in the army and stationed in the Pacific theater in World War 2. I saw him occasionally when I was growing up. My great-grandmother died in my first year of college. Neither experience caused me a great deal of emotional pain.

    After more weeks of my relentless grief, Michael finally sat me down and said, "Linda, this suffering is getting very old. I believe that you have repressed some deep hurt into your unconscious mind. You are acting like a trauma victim. I want to do some trance work to regress you back to that place, okay?" Michael has a master's degree in psychology and was trained as a psychotherapist. He is also an expert in hypnotherapy. I knew that I was in good hands. Several sessions later, we still had not discovered the underlying cause. Michael decided that I had a hypnotic block based on his previous experience of clients having them. After many sessions, the hypnotic block was released. I realized that the storyline in the movie was bringing up long forgotten childhood memories. E.T. was the key to helping Michael and me unlock the block that had been there my whole life. E.T. reminded me of friends who I had and lost. Michael and I recovered most of my memories while I was in trance. Some came in my dreams. For many weeks, I was lost in the memories of my past. This is the true story of my lost childhood told from my child's memories and in her voice.

    I lived on seven acres in Baltimore County in

Maryland. We had an orchard and large trees surrounding our old, white clapboard farmhouse. My mommy and I lived with my Aunt Marion, my Uncle Charles, and my sister, Sue. My uncle had a green thumb, and white rose bushes were everywhere. On the side of the house were four very tall, slender pine trees that created a perfect circle. I loved to play there. My collie, Lassie, and I made it our magical castle.

When I was 4, I decided to go outside to play at night. I wanted to see the stars, so I asked Aunt Marion if I could go. She said no, it was too late and getting chilly outside, and I needed to go to bed. She shooed me up the stairs, following with my favorite book in her hand. "I will read to you instead, and then you need to sleep," she said. I was not happy, but I let her put me to bed and listened to the book. I pretended to get sleepy, and she left my room, leaving the door ajar. I was in my pink and green flannel nightgown, so I knew I would be warm. I got up and quietly went down the stairs. Everyone was in the living room listening to the radio.

I heard a man's voice singing a beautiful song called "Linda." That is my name. I hummed along with it. They did not hear me go through the kitchen and out the back door.

Lassie was sleeping in the garage but woke up when I started patting her long hair. It was so soft and was the color of my hair. I thought she and I were sisters, each of us having long, blonde hair. We left the garage and followed the path to our magical circle. I smelled the roses and sat and looked at the stars. The moon was very big and very bright. Lassie and I looked at the stars until I got bored. I went to my little chest that I had hidden there and pulled out my favorite picture book.

The moonlight came through the trees and onto my pictures. Lassie and I were looking at the pictures of beautiful horses when I heard a soft, gentle noise coming from the top of the trees. I felt a little scared, but Lassie was very still, just listening. She was not scared. I listened too, waiting to see where the noise came from, and there they were: three balloons floating toward me. The noise went away, but there was a voice in my head telling me not to be afraid, that they were here to be my teachers.

"But I am too little to go to school," I said. "I am only 4 years old." The voice laughed. "We are not that kind of teachers."

For the next 5 years, I would pretend to sleepwalk and go outside. My Southern family had certain superstitions. One was to never wake a sleepwalker. I knew that and used it. I knew they watched me when I was in my circle, but they didn't "wake" me. Lassie and I sat and watched the bubbles moving around, and I listened to them inside my head.

They were my friends and teachers. I learned so much from them. They helped me understand how to read the feelings of sad and scared people by looking into their hearts and feeling what they felt. A lot of what they taught me did not come from words. I could feel a little tingling sensation in my head and heart, and I would laugh because it tickled me. They taught me how colors could make me feel happy and help when I was sad. They taught me to love nature and animals. I learned about how colors have different flavors, like ice cream, and meant different things. I learned about the stars and planets and how they were our friends.

One night, soon after I had met my friends, I felt scared when I was outside with them. Lassie snuggled up to me, protecting me. My friends were very kind and did what they could do to make me feel safe. One of them actually spread his bubble around Lassie and me, and I did feel a little better. Another friend said that he knew why I felt so scared. He asked if he could tell me about something that had occurred the year before. He said it was a scary story, but his friend still had us in his bubble.

"Okay," I said, "Will it make me feel better?"

"Yes, my child, it will help you understand what a brave, strong, and loving little girl you are. Remember Gary, who used to come here and mow the grass?"

I nodded. "Gary lived at the place my Mommy worked. People who were not very smart lived there. He liked to play with me sometimes."

My friend nodded and said, "Well, one day, the play got bad, and he hurt you. Your mother called the police. You were scared for him, not yourself. You told the police not to punish the young man because you were smarter than he was. You took responsibility for what happened, even though it was not your fault. You had sympathy for the boy and stood up for him. You were a very brave little girl, and you should be very proud of yourself. You weren't feeling scared then. So how do you feel now?"

"I remember," I said. "I felt sad for him and not scared, so why do I feel scared now?"

"Maybe you think it might happen again, and you wouldn't be as brave?" he said. That made sense to me.

Years later, when I was in the second grade, I watched as one of my classmates, Betsey, was being yelled at by our teacher, Mr. Ward. She was not listening to him and was talking to her friends in a loud voice. I knew that Mr. Ward was getting really angry at her. I walked up to his desk and asked to speak to him in the cloakroom outside the classroom. I remember that he was very surprised but said yes. I told him that Betsey was really just scared and needed someone to talk to her about that. I also said that she must have an angry father, and he had hurt her feelings many times. She didn't need to be yelled at by her teacher too. He looked at me like I was a crazy little girl.

"How on Earth do you know that?" he asked.

"Because I felt her heart!" I responded.

Shaking his head, he told me to go back to class. I sat down at my desk, scared that I was in big trouble. What if Mr. Ward started yelling at me? I wanted to tell Mr. Ward that my teachers had taught me how to feel people's problems, but I couldn't because they wanted their visits to be a secret. Mr. Ward was not mad at me, though. He smiled at me when he came back in the room. He stopped yelling at Betsey. He began being kind when he called on her, and Betsey a became a happier little girl.

Over the years, the bubbles were my best friends. I didn't have any "real" friends. I did not have a best friend. Aunt Marion had taught me to read by the time I was 4, so I was ahead of my classmates. I helped them with their homework so they would like me. I was different, so I guess they didn't know how to be with me. I wanted to be like everyone else and go to parties and sleepovers like all the other kids. That did not happen. I was a lonely, fat, little girl. My dog and my bubble friends were all that I had. They loved and accepted me for who I was. They knew that I was very smart and needed to learn.

My friends told me to read history books, especially Bruce Catton's books on the Civil War. He was a history writer. I had read them all by the time I was 9 years old. My family lived 45 minutes from Gettysburg, PA. Uncle Charles was a big fan of President Eisenhower. We spent many weekends at his farm in Gettysburg. My first memory was going to the battlefield when I was 3. We would find a picnic table where we could eat the nice lunch that my aunt made.

One day, I walked away from them to a spot that literally called to me. It was a little way from a stone wall. I went back and told Aunt Marion that I needed to sit on that spot and eat my lunch. She started to argue but then said okay. I guess she knew that I would be safe, because she could keep her eyes on me. This was before I could read and before my friends came. I shared this experience with my friends, and they told me to keep doing it. I did; I sat there each time we were in Gettysburg. Soon I began to be very sad when I sat there. I told my friends, and they told me that it would be better if I ate with my family. I didn't know why I was so interested in the Civil War. My teachers told me that one day, when I was older, I would figure it out.

There was so much they taught me. I didn't

understand much of it, yet I always went inside feeling happy and safe. They were my friends and they loved me. They helped me feel better about life. My stepfather was beginning to drink very heavily, and he and my mom would argue about that. He would be mad at all of us. Aunt Marion and my stepfather did not like each other, and she would tell me she would leave me if I called him "Daddy." I was scared all the time. I was in the middle of two warring adults and felt helpless. I had to sneak around them, being careful not to say the wrong thing.

When I was 9 years old, Lassie and I did our normal evening routine with my friends. That night, their bubbles were smaller and not as bright.

"What's wrong?" I asked, feeling a sense of real fear. "Please tell me. I know something is wrong. I am reading your hearts like you taught me."

One of the bubbles came close to me and stopped in front of my heart. Lassie growled, which scared me even more. She had never growled at them before.

My bubble friend said, "Lassie believes we are going to hurt you, and she is right. We must leave you now. You have to find ways to have real friends and live your life without us. We know you will be sad and feel angry at what we have to do. Someday you will understand. Please know we love you and I will always be with you. You will not see us or hear us, but we will help you as you grow up."

I sobbed, "No, please don't leave me. I need you so much. You are breaking my heart!" Lassie licked my tears, and we both watched as the bubbles disappeared.

The next few weeks were horrible. I cried all of the time. I was so sad and angry. Mom and Aunt Marion were helpless to console me. I ate all of the time. Aunt Marion baked my favorite cookies and made candy. She didn't know what else to do. I gained weight very fast. I tried to tell them about my friends and why I was so sad and cried so much. I told them they had to leave me and I was sad. They didn't believe me; they said I was making it up. That hurt even more and I ate more. I think I weighed 140 pounds when I was 9 years old. I had gained 40 pounds since my friends left. Between my weight and my sadness, everyone in my family was upset with me. Mom was scared that I would get sick if I didn't lose weight. I think Mom also felt bad when we were out and people looked at me funny. One day, as we were walking to our table in a restaurant, we overheard a lady telling her son, "See, if you eat too much, you could turn out to be just like her," pointing at me. I pretended I hadn't heard, but Mom did. She had a funny look on her face when we sat down.

    Later that week, Mom took me to see a doctor who, she said, could help me with my sadness and my weight. Mom took a day off from work, and we drove to the city. Normally, that would be an exciting adventure. I loved going to tea at a Baltimore department store and then shopping with my mom. But this trip was different. I was going to see a doctor, because there was something wrong with me. Mom and I sat in front of a big desk with a big man sitting behind it. He had a black beard, and I thought he looked like a bear. His voice was very soft and nice when he started talking to Mom. She told him about my friends and how she was scared that my imagination was taking over my life. She mentioned that I had gained so much weight and that I cried all the time.

    The doctor thanked her for talking to him and then asked her to leave us alone for a few minutes. "So, Linda, why don't you tell me about your friends," he asked in that soft voice. I told him everything. I told him about the nights with Lassie and me and my bubble friends. I told him what I had learned over the years and how I had helped people because I could read their hearts. I shared how sad I was when they left. I felt a little bad talking to him, because they had told me their visits were a secret, but I didn't care. I was angry at them for leaving.

    He wrote down what I said in a folder. When I was

finished, he smiled and said we would talk again soon. We talked once a week for a month or so. One day, he asked, "Many children have imaginary friends that help them through hard times. Do you think that maybe this is what you were doing?"

I sat there, thinking about how easy it would be to agree with the doctor so this nightmare would end. "Okay, doctor, you are probably right. They were my imagination. You are such a smart doctor. Thank you, I feel so much better!" I said this, knowing that he would be happy at my words and believe that I was okay, even though I knew I was lying.

"Linda, I am so glad you feel that way. Now you can make real friends. Now we need to work on your losing some weight, okay?" I nodded, knowing that I would not see this man again.

The next week, I told Mom that I was okay and that I didn't need to see the doctor again. I told her that I was happy and would be all right. She agreed, and I kept my sadness and anger to myself. One day at breakfast, my Aunt Marion asked if I had seen my "friends" lately. "What friends do you mean?" I responded. "I only have friends at school, and this is summer."

Thirty years later, I would realize that my bubble friends had visited me one more time and had blocked my memories of them. I now understood why they had done that. They had acted out of love and compassion for a little girl who had come to rely on them too much. The declaration I made then was to never become too open-hearted and vulnerable. That stayed with me until Michael and I removed the block.

I BECOME AN ASTROLOGER

My evolution into spiritual adulthood began when I started learning astrology. I met a man named Paul who was a trumpet player. We dated for a while, and he finally told me that he was interested in astrology. As a matter of fact, his first line to me had been, "You must be a Sagittarius. I have always been attracted to that sign." I did not know what he meant. "What is your birth date?" he continued, as I must have looked very confused.

"I was born December 13th," I replied.

"I knew it—you are a Sagittarian, and I bet you have Venus in Sag, too," he said, looking very pleased with himself. I remember laughing and changing the subject.

I liked him; he was talented and funny, but he never stopped talking about astrology. I thought astrology was stupid and silly and told him so often. We started to argue about it. One day, a totally frustrated Paul said, "When you know half as much as I do about astrology, we will talk again." I left in a huff and decided that I would research this and be better able to prove him wrong. The rest, of course is history. The more I learned, the most passionate I became to learn more. I discovered more about myself in my astrological studies than in 6 years of higher education in psychology and education. I never saw Paul again.

I was trained in experimental psychology and behavior modification. I believed in what could be measured, analyzed, and charted. I also believed in Christ, the Episcopal church, and its mysteries in a childlike, naive way. I did not question. I had faith, but life has a way of intruding on faith, and mine did not stand the test. I began my study of astrology in an earnest quest to disprove it, but I found instead that it gave me answers. Even more important, it gave me questions. The idea that the stars wielded the energy to create the perfect chart for me had always made me uncomfortable. It meant that I was not in control of my life and that I could blame the stars for my problems, including my struggles with my weight. As my understanding of astrology grew, however, the answer became quite clear: My soul had created my astrological chart.

Years later, I resigned my position as a vice principal to become a professional astrologer. My soul knew the symbolic meanings of all the astrological signs and planets and the relationships between them. It had created an astrological mandala to provide me with the tools I needed to experience my life. My soul knew my past; it had been there. My soul knew what this life needed to be as a continuation of what was left from other lives. My soul, in other words, understood my karma. When our souls choose our charts, they give us an opportunity to learn about the diverse parts of ourselves. I finally discovered why my childhood bubble friends wanted me to read all of the Civil War books and why my little girl needed to eat her lunch in front of the stone wall at Gettysburg. I had been a Southern general who had died

100 yards from the angle. Exactly where I sat for so many years when I was a little girl.

DISCOVERING MY INNER CHILD

Remembering Carl Jung's theory, I finally realized that I had repressed all knowledge of my childhood and the young part of me—my inner child. The chaos she created was becoming dangerous to my emotional and physical health. It was then that I understood why I was so distressed over the child abuse epidemic. In my ignorance, I was abusing a child: my own little inner child! I had repressed the memory of her and literally abandoned her for years. From her hidden, unconscious home, she was feeling all of my unconscious emotions and being damaged by them. Every time I judged myself as being unworthy or failing at something, my little inner child heard that too. Worse than that, she believed what I said and bore the emotional impact of my self-contempt. She heard and believed, about herself, all the denigrating and demeaning things that I said about myself. She remembered the rape and the loss of her friends as if it were yesterday.

She carried the burden of all of that pain. She ate sweets to numb all of the hurts and to find some sweetness in her life.

It didn't matter to her how fat I was. She was taking care of herself. As a matter of fact, she was probably afraid that if I were thin and pretty, I would be raped again. That was the reality she lived with every day.

One day, in my frustration with her, I told her she was killing me. Then, I remembered a moment when I was 7 years old. My mother and I were outside, pruning a white country rose bush, when I turned to her and asked "Mommy, when do I get to go home?" She looked surprised and answered, "Honey, you are home." "No," I replied, "my real home. Heaven." My mother quickly changed the subject. My little girl still wanted to go home, so she was not worried about killing me. She was, in fact, passively suicidal. This was a significant wake-up for me. I would have to find ways to understand and change her deep beliefs about living on Earth.

Lynnie Becomes Real

I did not know my inner child as a real part of me. Intellectually, I knew that I had unconscious memories that were imprinted at the young age of 3. It did not occur to me that she was a real, breathing little girl who was hiding away from me for her own emotional reasons. My soul had other plans. It helped me learn the reality of my inner child. It created several powerful situations that helped me see, feel, hear, and touch the reality of my inner little girl. One of those important plans was for me to become an astrologer. Learning the signs, planets, and houses of my chart gave me all of the information I needed to understand her.

"The child is in me still and sometimes not so still."

—**Fred Rogers**

On a beautiful day, while walking in the town of Celebration, Florida, my husband and I heard a childlike voice loudly say, "I hate baby poopy pink and baby poopy blue, too." After looking around and seeing no one else near us, we laughed. It was Lynnie, my inner child, giving us her firm opinion about pale pink and blue. Her words were totally spontaneous and potentially humiliating, if they had been spoken in a busy environment where other people could hear them. Have you ever said or done something so automatic that it surprised and embarrassed you? Well, look over your shoulder, and you may discover the voice of your child. We are often at the mercy of this unconscious part of our selves. This was Carl Jung's unconscious projection theory in spades. My unconscious child was making herself known to me in what could have been an embarrassing event.

Lynnie and I had an emotional episode a few years ago after I took a Reiki class. I had helped a man heal his lower back pain by putting my hands on him. That event should have brought me happiness, but instead I started to feel depressed. The next week, I had a client who experienced chronic headaches. She, too, wanted hands-on healing, because I had done it before and it worked temporarily. I suggested that we try a new strategy. Using her astrological chart, I was able to ask important questions that helped her see the true core causation of her headaches. Two days later, my client called, reporting that the headaches had not returned. She was overjoyed, and I hung up the phone in tears. I was totally confused about the feelings that both of those healing sessions had catalyzed.

It finally occurred to me that it was not my adult self but my inner child, Lynnie, sharing her feelings to me. I asked her what was wrong. She cried, "Jesus doesn't love you!"

"Why?" I asked, totally stunned.

"Because Jesus was a healer, and He touched people and made them well. You helped that man, and it made me sad you had not been doing that very much. And then you wouldn't help that lady with her headache. We are not doing what Jesus wants us to do, and we are going to Hell!"

Wow, that was a shock! Lynnie wanted me to emulate Jesus, and nothing would change her mind about how I should do my work. It took me weeks to help her see that it was important to teach the lady how to cure herself. Often, Lynnie would shake her little head "no." She was still remembering and feeling the young Southern Baptist that she had been taught to be. She believed in Heaven and Hell, right and wrong, good and evil. She loved Jesus and wanted us to emulate Him—period! We have come a long way from those days, and we still have conversations about what it is like for me to be a new-age Christian. Over time, she has watched me help thousands of people during my 43 years in practice. She is happy about that and now believes we are going to Heaven.

The final experience that convinced me of her reality

occurred when I decided to have a tummy tuck to repair the damage caused by being obese for so many years. The surgery was planned a year in advance. For several months preceding the operation, I talked about it to my inner child, Lynnie. I promised her that she would not be hurt and that she would be in the safe arms of my husband ("Mikey") during the surgery. I believed that I had done enough and that she would be fine. I arrived at the clinic half an hour early, excited, and a bit nervous. I checked in with the nurse, exchanged some chit-chat, and sat down with my husband to wait for the intake nurse. Then, seemingly out of nowhere, I became hysterical, crying so hard that I could not breathe. The nurse and Michael tried to comfort me and get me to calm down.

My doctor came out and talked to me. He looked at me with deep concern, clearly in doubt of whether he should operate. The adult part of me knew that he was thinking about canceling it. I wanted that surgery! I was experiencing back problems because my body was off balance, I never had a flat stomach, and I didn't think that I could maintain my weight loss with such apparent evidence of my obesity still clinging to my body—yet I could not stop crying. I begged the surgeon to give me a few minutes to get myself together. He agreed. He had performed other procedures on me and knew who I was, mentally, physically and most of all, spiritually.

Finding the Safe Place

I went into the bathroom. I sat in the stall, asking my soul for help. Through the tears, I heard a little voice screaming at me: "Mommy, Mommy, you are taking my hiding place away. I'm so scared. Why are you doing this to me? It is my safe place." The shock of this stopped the tears, and I listened to my dear little inner child tell me how scared she was. I truly felt her; she was really there.

I thought about all of the perfunctory talks I had had with her leading up to this day. I had done all of the talking and was pretty pleased with myself for taking care of her. Truth be told, I was taking care of myself, not Lynnie. There I was, sitting on a toilet, totally unprepared for what was happening. I did notice that I—the adult me—was calmer. Okay, I said to myself, talk to this little child and help her. I took a deep breath and told Lynnie that I would not have the surgery if we could not figure out together what to do to make her safe. That quieted her. She knew from our years of communication that I never consciously lied to her.

"So," I said, "what if we could move your home somewhere else in my body?" She asked, "Where?"

"How about my heart?" I asked.

She cried, "NO, NO!!! TOO SCARED THERE!"

Wow, I had not expected that! It made perfect sense, though. My heart connects me to my world, my husband, my dogs, my friends, and my clients. She was right; that would be a very vulnerable place for her to be, unless... unless I could promise her that I would totally protect her there. That would take total consciousness. Could I really promise that? Time was running out. I had to either make that promise to my little girl or cancel the surgery.

I decided to tell her that I would take care of her in my heart and that she could trust me. We talked about her spending more time in her beautiful sanctuary with her dogs and toys and Aunt Marion when it would be impossible for me to take care of her. That made her smile. "I love them," she said, her voice steadier now. "Okay, that is what we will do," I said. I hugged her and I had the surgery. My recovery was fast and uneventful. I was walking four miles a day within a month.

Anne's Experience

Years ago, I received a call from a young father from Arizona. John was terrified that his wife, Anne, would hurt his newborn son. She was diagnosed with postpartum depression and had been medicated by her doctor. Nothing had really changed, except she was worried about the effects the drugs would have on her milk and, through that, her baby. He put Anne on the call. She was frantic and sobbing. I could barely understand her.

"Mrs. Brady," she cried, "I thought about putting a pillow over my baby's head today. I didn't know what I was doing. John came into the room and stopped me. Please help me, I don't want to hurt my baby."

"Okay," I responded quietly. "Is your husband still there? I would like to talk to him too." John got on the phone and put them on speaker. "Okay, John, are you off work?" I asked.

"Yes, I have 3 more weeks of leave," he said wearily.

"Great," I said, "so you can take over some baby care while I work with Anne, right?

After a brief silence, John said he would do that. "Can

46

you really help Anne?" John asked. "The treatment she has had is not working."

"I have an idea," I responded. "I am doing inner child work with many of my clients. Getting in touch with her little internal child could help. I am willing to try." I had seen in many client experiences that inner children do not like their mommy paying attention to external children, if not to them. That's why there's a lot of postpartum depression: The Inner Child gets angry and depressed when there is another child. It's like, "Mommy is paying attention to this baby and not to me. Well, I don't like this baby." Two weeks later, Anne was conscious of her inner child. She was embracing and honoring her little girl and dealing with her child's rage at the new baby. She learned that loving and embracing her inner child was just as important as loving her new baby.

Anne believed that she was a one-trick pony. She was either going to be a good or bad mother; there was no other option. She had no idea how complicated she was. In these moments after the birth of her child, she was operating from a very young, dangerous place. Her inner child was in charge of her life without her even knowing it. Her inner child was totally unconscious, and its jealousy and anger created Anne's life to be out of control and chaotic. We've all had moments when we said or did something that, afterward, we could not believe we said or did. These behaviors are immature and childish. We all experience moments of being very self-centered, having temper tantrums, or other extreme behaviors. Therefore, our inner children can be impulsive, extreme, and emotionally chaotic. I've had clients whose lives were controlled by their inner children. When our inner child is driving the car, we can expect accidents along our way.

CHILDHOOD EMOTIONAL DECLARATIONS

"Let us not get scooped up by gaslighting manipulators stealing our emotions and taking possession of our inner child to carry out their dark agenda. Let the light of our intuition guide us subtly and wisely along the path of trust and suspicion. ("Juicy rumors")"

— Erik Pevernagie

"I'm not so sure that the adult within me teaches the child within me. Rather, I think that the child does most of the educating."

— Craig D. Lounsbrough

"When our inner child is not nurtured and nourished, our minds gradually close to new ideas, unprofitable commitments and the surprises of the Spirit."

—Brennan Mann

"Let us listen to the needs of our inner child that is being tamed and imprisoned by the rules of a grown-up world. ("Going back to yesterday")"

— Erik Pevernagie

49

We all have emotionally charged experiences that become powerful emotional mantras that repeat themselves over and over until they become conscious. They end up controlling your life. Determining your unconscious, emotional declarations is critically important in altering your life's experiences. One of the most important reasons to do inner child work is that it helps us to become whole individuals. To be a whole, integrated person, we also need to take care of parts of ourselves that are not apparent to us because they reside in our unconscious mind. Yes! It goes back to the Jungian thing, "What we repress within ourselves, we create outside of ourselves as chaos." Our inner children create a lot of chaos in our lives because they're unconscious—especially if they're emotionally challenged. My little girl made an emotional declaration when her friends left her. She vowed at 9 years old to never be emotionally vulnerable and trust anyone who could abandoned her. She, in essence, turned her emotions off. That contaminated her life for years.

Mark's Story

Mark and his young family have been clients and friends for many years. I married him and his lovely wife, Lynn, and baptized their two children. They did premarital coaching and saw Michael and me on and off when situations arose. One day, I received a call from Lynn, telling us that their daughter, Gloria, had requested talking to Michael and me because she had "issues." We smiled at that because she was 8 years old, sounding like a psychologically aware adult. We happily honored her request and began half-hour weekly coaching sessions with her. Then, the family took an eagerly awaited trip to North Carolina to visit with Mark's father.

Two weeks later, Lynn called with very upsetting news that Gloria had been sexually molested by Mark's father. Many sessions later, Gloria, who had been very clear about her feelings, was beginning to heal. Mark, on the other hand, was not. He was understandably angry and sad about what had happened to his precious little girl. As a police officer, he was conflicted about his feelings and what further actions to take. As a father, he was obsessed with shame and guilt that it was his fault. Nothing Michael, Lynn, or I said seemed to make a difference. Finally, it occurred to me that this was not just about Gloria: It was about himself.

When Mark was 8 years old, the same age as Gloria, his father left the family. Through meditation, we took Mark back to that day. He saw his little boy watching his daddy leave. With tears in his eyes and a clenched fist, he screamed inside his head, "I WILL NEVER LEAVE MY FAMILY!" I WILL NOT BE LIKE MY DADDY! He was 8 years old, creating an emotional declaration that would be in control of his life for 22 years. He was making an impassioned statement that was causing him great distress now. His inner child felt that he had failed. He had not taken care of his family. The guilt and shame were overwhelming. Mark realized that emotional declaration was coming from his inner child and not his adult self. With tears running down his face, he made a commitment to his inner little boy that he was always going to be his good daddy. He would never leave and abandon him. The pain of that abandonment was becoming healed. The whole family is staying committed to regular coaching and are doing great!

These young childhood emotional declarations need to be made conscious. Understanding the contaminated emotions of your inner child will create a clarity and freedom necessary for a happy life. Think about a life situation where this may be true for you.

Your Early Declarations and Their Impact

Please record your thoughts and feelings in the space provided below.

_____

_____

_____

_____

_____

_____

_____

_____

_____

_____

_____

_____

_____

COMMUNICATION: THE KEY TO UNDERSTANDING YOUR INNER CHILD

One of the first things I tell my new interns is that it is our responsibility to hear, understand, and communicate effectively with our clients. To do that, I tell them, they must learn and master the symbols, meanings, and energies of all 12 astrological signs. You can imagine their reaction upon learning that they must master 12 languages! However, acknowledging that there are 12 different ways to perceive and process information is the philosophical underpinning on which the study of Mercury is based. Considering that people's views of the world are influenced by 12 different spiritual filters, compounded by their religious, racial, and ethnic contexts, the enduring conflagrations across the globe become easier to comprehend, if not less distressing. Communicating effectively is one of our highest priorities, paramount to the success of all our relationships, yet few people understand that there are 12 different ways to do it..

Learning about your personal filter—your Mercury's traits—and the filters of those people with whom you interact undoubtedly will be one of the most essential lessons you glean from this book. Mercury differs from the other planets in that it is not a karmic planet. It deals only with issues relating to our personality in this life. Your Mercury filter was chosen for you by your soul for your personality's intellectual evolution.

    Each of you has a sign into which the planet Mercury is located at the time of your birth. Being able to communicate with your outer world is critical to your life. Learning how to be a great parent to your inner child depends on how you communicate with them, too. Words are power, as you have observed in childhood declarations! The impact of their personal filter—their Mercury placement—transcends all of the effects manifested in them by their nationality, race, gender, and so on. Mercury is about who children are, how they receive and perceive information, what they do with it, and how they express themselves once they have it. Mercury symbolizes the way they indigenously comprehend the world at large within the context of their own lives. Children of the same parents, raised in the same home, attending the same school, and trained in the same religious and social environments, can be extraordinarily different in how they filter their world. Mercury helps them understand their intellectual and emotional orientations to life, showing how they communicate their innate talents and connect with others. It defines how they wish to align themselves with others by sharing their ideas, thoughts, and ideals. It represents their desire to express their needs, perceptions, and ideas through speech, as well as their need to be understood.

I divide Mercury traits into two categories: receptive (receiving information) and expressive (giving information). There are 12 different ways to perceive and process information; this is the philosophical underpinning on which the study of Mercury is based. Please locate your Mercury placement from your chart by its sign and glyph in the Addendum or in your packet of information.

The Four Filters and Their Elements

Although the characteristics of the 12 signs are widely disparate, they can be classified into four general groups based on some shared similarities: Earth, Fire, Air, and Water. Since the four elements are the foundations of the natural world, they manifest in the heavens through the astrological signs. For example, the Earth element reflects Earth energy in the heavens through the constellations of Taurus, Virgo, and Capricorn; Water reflects its energy through Cancer, Scorpio, and Pisces; Air reflects its energy through Gemini, Libra, and Aquarius; and Fire reflects its energy through Aries, Leo, and Sagittarius. Each of the elements symbolizes a general temperament. For instance,

Earth signs are concrete, practical, material, and sensation oriented. Water signs are emotional, intuitional, sensitive, and creative. Air signs are intellectual, communicative, and relational. Fire signs are action oriented, willful, inspirational, and spontaneous. The totality of the four groups is the human personality. Mercury takes on the basic temperament of the element in which it is placed. Once you've looked up the sign of your Mercury placement, consult the elements chart to determine the type of filter your inner child possesses and how it influences the way your child receives, processes, and expresses information.

Mercury in Earth: Taurus, Virgo, and Capricorn

- Ideas and thoughts are practical, determined, visual, and concrete.

- Learning is best accomplished through the five senses: visual, auditory, tactile, kinesthetic, and olfactory.

- Filter is earthy and sensational, focused on the senses.

- Communication is persistent, specific, cautious, and patient.

- Thought processes are shaped by practical realities and traditional material concerns.

Mercury in Water: Cancer, Scorpio, and Pisces

- Ideas and thoughts are influenced by deeply felt emotions.

- Learning is best accomplished by being creative, intuitional, and sensitive.

- Filter is the feeling and desire for emotional connectedness.

- Communication is emotional, empathic, intuitional, sometimes psychic, and withheld and evasive if strong emotions are present.

- Thought processes are shaped by emotional and intuitional concerns.

Mercury in Air: Gemini, Libra, and Aquarius

- Ideas and thoughts are important in and of themselves.

- Learning is best accomplished by gathering information about many different ideals and social and environmental situations.

- Filter is based on curiosity and versatility.

- Communication is versatile, socially adept, articulate, innovative, and objective.

- Thought processes are shaped by a love of sharing ideas.

Mercury in Fire: Aries, Leo, and Sagittarius

- Ideas and thoughts are influenced by future visions, philosophy, beliefs, and hopes.

- Learning is best accomplished through understanding abstract concepts or the bigger picture, as well as by taking action assertively.

- Filter is the need to have insight, to understand the gestalts of life.

- Communication is powerful, inspirational, assertive, quick, spontaneous, and enthusiastic.

- Thought processes are shaped by sharing inspired philosophical beliefs.

The Four Filters at Work in the Classroom

As a former administrator in education, I remain fascinated with the way children communicate. It is equally important to understand how you need to talk to your inner child. I was very fortunate to be introduced to the teachers and administrators of two fine private schools. One teacher invited me to come to her third-grade class for Career Day. I used it as an opportunity to introduce the children to their Mercury placements. It was the first time that I had grouped children by Mercury. I divided them into groups according to the four elements. Soon, they began to develop relationships between themselves and their element's filter. They talked about "their" element as if it were their best friend. They laughed and discussed how the members of their own group were so alike. Then I did some role-playing, using a stuffed dog as a prop.

    I would like you to imagine your inner child in this classroom. Using your Mercury sign and its element, see how your inner child can relate to in my role-playing game. Discover strategies you may use to communicate with your inner child's Mercury and its elemental. I had a child with Mercury in Air discuss the dog with a child who had Mercury in Water. The Air child, because of her orientation toward wanting to share ideas, told the Water child that she wanted to name the dog. The Water child, with her filter skewed toward emotion, wanted to love the dog, hug the dog, and pet it. The Air child became a little annoyed and started listing possible names. The Water child shrugged and continued to hug the stuffed animal. There was virtually no communication between the two children. What happened? The Air child's filter to the world was to think about it and label it.

That's what Air Mercuries do: They're interested in words, in labeling, articulating, and classifying things by description. Naming the dog was important to her, but expressing her opinion to the Water child was equally important. She wanted an intellectual exchange to find the right name. By contrast, the Water child's filter was to perceive the world through feelings and to express herself emotionally. She wanted to connect with the stuffed animal and did. She was unable to identify with the Air child on an emotional level, so she put her feelings where she could: on the dog. I then had two more children do the same role-playing with the dog, except this time, one little girl had a Fire Mercury, and the other had an Earth Mercury.

    The Fire child took the dog from me, put it on the floor, and pretended to walk it. She wanted the Earth Mercury to walk it with her. The Earth child did not respond. Getting bored, the Fire child began to play catch with it. Consistent with the characteristics of Fire in Mercury, the Fire child's first two impulses upon seeing the dog were to take action in some way. The Earth child reached down and took the dog and began to pet it. She needed to have the dog in her possession. She was interested in the dog's coat and its texture. She told the Fire child how soft the dog's fur was. The Fire child took the dog and again played catch with it. This bothered the Earth child, who wanted to pet it. Once again, there was no communication between the children.

    Before resuming the role-playing, I talked to all four girls about their experiences and their inherent differences, and then I coached them to help them create alignment in their interaction. I reminded the Air child that her friend, "Water," was more interested in feelings than thoughts. I asked her to think about and share her emotions about the dog, even though that wasn't her first reaction. I told the Air child that if she wanted to talk to her friend, she would have to use words her friend could understand. So "Air" told "Water" that she "felt happy" when she held the dog and then asked "Water" how she felt. "Water" responded by agreeing that she also felt happy when she held the dog. Then, I asked the Water child to pay attention to her feelings after talking with "Air." She told me she was happy because "Air" was "interested" in her feelings. After I reminded her, the Water child was able to cooperate with the Air child about what she needed.

I used the same coaching technique to reach the Fire and Earth children. All I had to do was to remind each one of the other's needs. I told the Fire child how important touching was to the Earth child, and she suggested that the Earth child "hold the dog." In turn, I reminded the Earth child that doing something was important to "Fire." Because the Earth child was secure with having the dog in her possession, she was able to participate in "Fire's" game. In turn, the Fire child was happy because she was able to create some new action—an imaginary three-way game of catch—for both of them to enjoy. "Earth" happily complied. "Fire" threw a make-believe ball to the dog, and "Earth" caught the "ball" from the dog and threw it back to "Fire."

Your Response

Your Inner Child's Mercury

The Mercury placement in your astrological chart gives you very specific, practical information in how you need to communicate with your inner child. Many of my clients are confused about why and how they need to talk to their inner child. The "why" is because your inner child is emotionally receptive to hearing you from his or her birth. The "how" is: Describe using the descriptors that I have provided you. Locate yours by discovering your Mercury sign and writing it here: _____. Read and then record with your personal responses.

Mercury in Aries

Your inner child seeks to understand the world as an exciting reality to be explored and conquered. They want to be confident that they are strong, assertive, and independent.

They naturally believe that, through their self-awareness and creativity, they can make anything happen. Your inner child welcomes physical challenges and usually rises to the top because of their physical strength, will, and agility. They want you to talk to them about your courageous ideas and your love of exploration and adventure. They want to feel your excitement of creating new beginnings. Your child might be impatient if their life is moving too slowly. They want their life to be a series of new beginnings and can be easily distracted and bored if it is not.

Provide them opportunities to take actions, especially physically challenging ones. it. Find creative outlets to foster self-awareness, self-esteem, and self-value. Be careful that you are not impulsive in your speaking to them. Do not diminish their emotional reactions to anger. They know that they can be angry and want to learn how to handle it. They need you to help them find creative techniques to transform their anger into excitement, joy and enthusiasm.

Your Response

Mercury in Taurus

Your inner child sees and feels the world as a creative garden that they want to seed and see grow in their life. They desire material security and creating physical bonds with the earth on many different levels. Because they value consistency, they build their earthy life cautiously, carefully, and conservatively. They tend their spiritual and physical garden one step at a time, so that it will flourish. Honor their patience and determination to finish their projects. Provide opportunities for them to see the quality and practical value in what they create.

You know they need serenity and calm and help them find that in their daily life. You want to help them find ways to make changes when they are likely to remain stuck. They speak in a slow, methodical fashion to make sure that their ideas will be understood. They communicate these ideas and thoughts in words that are practical and conservative. They tend to create pictures with their words because of their desire to use all of their physical senses. When they argue with you, help them find creative ways to find a new perspective. They can then take actions to resolve the underlying issues.

Your Response

Mercury in Gemini

Your inner child is an information gatherer. Their inner life is a library filled with new ideas, thoughts, and experiences to satisfy their insatiable curiosity. They are mentally alert and are quick to grasp a new idea. They love words and language and are avid readers and writers. Your inner child responds to the world with mental agility, brightness, and cleverness. They speak eloquently with flair and excitement. These inner children cleverly put different words together and are known for their creative use of language. They often do more than one thing at a time: watching TV, reading a book, and talking on the phone.

When they become distracted and speak in vague and confusing patterns, you need to help them focus and prioritize. Provide them opportunities to write down their goals instead of keeping everything in their mind. Help them understand the importance of emotions when they seem restless and not grounded. Teach them the power of nature, and allow your mind energy to connect to the earth. Help them choose inspirational, broader concept words to focus on the big expansive perspective of the meaning of life.

Your Response

Mercury in Cancer

Your child is an emotionally sensitive nurturer and the archetypical mother. They would like the world to be their extended home to provide every one with the foundations, support, and security. They listen by paying close attention to their emotional environment. If the words they hear do not mesh with the emotions they sense, they will ignore those words. Emotions color all of their perceptions and thoughts. Your inner child may lose their emotional identity because of their highly developed empathy to others. Their speech is emotional, caring, and nurturing, as they are being sympathetic and supportive in their relationships. They want to talk about their home and family and about the past.

You want to teach them not to bring old past emotional issues into their present. Honor how they want to communicate through actions like cooking, finding a sentimental greeting card, or being emotionally present when someone is in pain. Listen to them when they share their need to close down emotionally. Provide them alternatives when they get scared or intimidated. Help them create good boundaries when they are too empathetic and sensitive. Teaching them to look at situations from a practical, earthy, less emotional perspective will also help.

Your Response

Mercury in Leo

Your child sees the world as a stage on which they dramatically perform their life. They watch for opportunities to be on center stage and obtain the applause they feel is necessary for their happiness. They perceive the world from their heart, needing relationships that will enhance their sense of dignity and acknowledgment. Your inner child finds fun, excitement, and childlike wonder in their speech, which has a strong dramatic, self-confident flair. They are commanding and self-assured in their communication. Provide them opportunities to find their pride and dignity as you create a heart-to-heart connection with them.

You want to understand their need to receive admiration, praise, and approval. At the same time, reminding them that self-honor and self-respect will make them happier and stronger. Pay attention when they seem dominating and self-absorbed, as this is a sign of insecurity and vulnerability. Teaching them to connect with their heart center will create self-love. Provide opportunities for them to inspire others and be more connected to their natural leadership.

Your Response

Mercury in Virgo

Your inner child perceives the world as a giant jigsaw puzzle to be put together and organized. Their world, then, is a complex system of thought, work, and service needing structure and order. Because they consider themselves the right person to create this systematic environment, they become its efficient, concerned promoter. They believe in its intrinsic, earthly perfection. Your inner child wants to maintain high standards through their methodical, logical, analytical style. They look for ways to create healthy physical systems for themselves and others. They use their powers of discrimination to find ways to be of service to those who request it. They are exacting and seek to bring coherence to the world. Their speech is clear, analytical, discriminating, and exact. They are devoted to organizing their speech to be practical, efficient, and precise. Their propensity for inductive reasoning shows through their words and expressed thoughts.

Much of their language involves health issues, work habits and environment, and a need for order. They are interested in fixing situations you consider broken. They can be judgmental, critical, and extreme in their speech. Because their standards are so high, you can appear as a worried, anxious communicator. They can be obsessed with very small details, putting their life in boxes. They can be too analytical and perfectionistic. Overcoming their challenges and changing their orientation to perfection is critical to overcoming their challenges. Realizing the intrinsic perfection of their deep self will keep them from worrying about external perfection. Strive for excellence, not perfection. Teach them to be gentle and compassionate with themselves when they are inclined to be anxious about doing things right. Be cognizant of their extreme expectations, and be more creative in finding third options.

Your Response

Mercury in Libra

Your inner child sees the world as a cosmic courtroom, with you as the benevolent judge. They abhor injustice and unfairness. They seek refinement, beauty, balance, and harmony in the world. Their world is a web of social relationships that need mediation and arbitration, through their skills of cooperation and need for justice. They perceive both sides of all arguments and endeavor to find the balanced center and middle ground. Your inner child wants to see a socially refined and charming world. Their speech is diplomatic, cultured, and socially oriented. They can be charming, affectionate, and persuasive in their words. They express thoughts that produce compromise and negotiation in social situations. Their actions, as much a part of their communication as words, seek to please, to avoid conflict, and to create beautiful surroundings. They can be too flattering of others because they do not wish to hurt anyone's feelings. They compromise so much that, at times, they compromise themselves and are more interested in others' needs than their own.

They can be superficial and too interested in what other people think of them. Their desperate need to find balance and harmony can mire them in indecision and ambivalence. They care about pleasing others, sometimes at the expense of themselves. You need to teach them to think about themselves as an important relationship in addition to all your external relationships. Provide them opportunities to say "no" on occasion. Help them learn that being present in conflicts is important. Conflicts create opportunities to find a third option, which is usually the most valuable. Coach them in how to take an action on an issue in which they would normally be indecisive and ambivalent.

Your Response

Mercury in Scorpio

Your inner child is an emotional investigator seeking intensity and passion—even emotional chaos—to find the deeper understanding of what they desire. Their thoughts and ideas are colored by their emotional needs to probe human psychology. They respect and attract all forms of courage. They see the world as exciting, intriguing, and somewhat dangerous. Their speech is tinged with emotional intensity and a need for internal power. They are extreme; their all-or-nothing attitude is evident in their words as well as in their expressed ideas and thoughts. They are passionate about their beliefs and are not afraid to articulate them to others. Their speech can be intimidating and frightening to those less intense than them. They can be relentless in their quest to sort out the mysteries of life—especially death and sexuality—and they seek to communicate their ideas frequently. Because they can be extreme, they can also withhold communication and appear to be cold and emotionally withdrawn.

Your inner child may have a tendency to want to be in control of their communication. They may only hear words that are filtered through intense emotions. Because they can feel your intentions and motivations, be emotionally present and be honest. It is important for you to coach them into finding ways to be less extreme by showing them the power of third options. They will need you to model what patience and serenity looks like. Gardening can help, because it will modulate their intensity and focus.

Your Response

_____

_____

_____

_____

_____

_____

_____

Mercury in Sagittarius

Your child is a young philosopher, seeing the world as a giant cornucopia of boundless opportunities and knowledge. Nature becomes the symbol for freedom, expansion, the natural order, and experience. They learn, through the explicate order of nature, how things work. Through it, they see and learn about serendipity, prosperity, joy, and survival. They learn best by experiencing life, not just thinking or talking about it. They see the highest potential in all people through their filter of faith, hope, and optimism. Your child speaks as a teacher and a philosopher, exploring abstract ideas. They perceive the world as something to be experienced, without boundary or restriction. All things are possible as long as they have enough faith. They wish to discover the truth so they can share it and teach it to others. Your child is the spiritual visionary and teacher, creating goals that are idealistic and devotional.

You need to speak with your inner child with honesty and openness. They can intuit a lie or secrets, and this makes them distrustful and scared. Honor their enthusiasm, and encourage their search for enlightenment with every step they take. They easily communicate with nature and animals, so give them plenty of opportunities to discover its magic. You notice that they want to teach people around them, so encourage them to find ways to do that. They need to learn to listen as well as speak. Admonish them not to be too direct in their communication. They can be a bit too pedantic, believing that their truth is the only truth. Encourage them to gather information before being too dogmatic. Your inner child believes in the power of faith, and you need to support that.

Your Response

Mercury in Capricorn

Your inner child appears to be an old, wise adult, wanting their world to be a place of practical, traditional reality. They seek reality in thought and action and are methodical in how they view the world. They are disciplined and reserved, careful and cautious in their judgment of how things work. They want to impose their responsible organizational nature on life's inconsistencies. Your inner child looks at the ladder of life and wants to climb to the top. They value the world's material bounty and want to claim it. Their speech is conservative and reserved. They think long and hard before they speak. Their words are practical, realistic, and mature. They have excellent common sense. They incorporate their respect for history and traditions into their thoughts and words. They prepare for any verbal presentation thoroughly, because they take their communication seriously. They have an avuncular way. They tend to speak about self-reliance, honor, and respect. They will be an excellent disciplinarian and leader. However, they may be inflexible and intolerant of views that seem too far-fetched for them. Their rigidity may make them judgmental of others' views.

You need to encourage your inner child's wisdom and bias to being personally responsible. They can be pessimistic, seeing life's failures rather than its successes. Teach them to be more whimsical, carefree, and enthusiastic. Provide them opportunities to connect with their emotions that will help them be more relaxed and feel less external pressure. Work on helping them access their emotions as well as your beliefs. Work on becoming more relaxed and optimistic. Be cognizant of your child's tendency toward rigidity; figure out what it represents, and help them create more flexibility. Make an effort to allow your inner child opportunities to lighten up and be more childlike.

Your Response

Mercury in Aquarius

Your inner child sees the world as a place filled with innovation and invention, with a rational divine order to the universe. They think that all things that occur in life have a reason, although they may not always understand them. Accepting others' differences, they value individuals for their innovation and uniqueness. They search for global tolerance, cooperation, and humanitarianism. They see future possibilities and invent new technologies to improve the human condition. With a broad philosophical outlook, they naturally understand the New Age triangle of mind, body, and soul. They seek equality and gravitate toward like-minded groups that share their reformer's vision. They are a highly innovative thinker and communicator. They are intuitional in what they say and how they say it, valuing and speaking about equality. Your inner child has a predilection toward high tech, computers, science, and New Age philosophy. They are humanistic and talk about how one person can make a difference. However, they can be erratic and eccentric at times, as well as a bit rebellious.

Your inner child can be detached and remote. It is as their minds are somewhere else. It may be because they have a strong inner life and are often thinking about things others may not understand. Honor their expertise with computers, and work on speaking their unique language. They are very bright and approach life from an intelligent point of view. You might want to teach them about their emotions and the power of rationality. They may become obsessed with games and attract like-minded friends who want to become part of their circle. Talk to them about humanism, and find opportunities for them to become involved in causes they might enjoy.

Your Response

Mercury in Pisces

Your inner child is a spiritual romantic, wanting the world to be beautiful, sensitive, and loving. They seek the creative, the poetic, the lyrical. Their psychic, intuitive nature wants to make the world a more spiritual place. Their thoughts and ideas are colored by their deep emotional desire for compassion and love. Your inner child is a sensitive, intuitional communicator. Your language is gentle, loving, spiritual, and creative. They express their ideas and thoughts carefully, so as not to hurt anyone's feelings, and because they are so perceptive and intuitional, they know what to say and how to say it. However, this may mean that they are not entirely honest in how they express their own wants and needs. Your inner child expresses their poetic and romantic feelings when they feel safe. Otherwise, they can be very quiet and shy. Because they are so sensitive to others' feelings, they can alter their own emotions very quickly to match the others. They may appear moody and inconsistent.

Your inner child needs you to speak gently and lovingly to them. They will empathize with your feelings and want to make sure that you are okay. They will sacrifice their own needs to satisfy yours. Teach them that their wants are important too, and help them find boundaries to protect them. Encourage them to be as gentle and compassionate with themselves as they are with others. Let them know that they can be assertive and say "no" occasionally. Create opportunities for them to express what they want. Support their creative love of music and dance. They understand emotion, so assist them in becoming a master of theirs. They want to talk about spiritual matters and are very intuitional.

Your Response

YOUR EMOTIONAL INNER CHILD

"Some people think ignoring their inner child makes them seem grown-up. When I see someone ignoring a crying child, I think they're an asshole."

—**Jay Bell**

Thirty years ago, I was teaching an astrological class about the Moon. I was standing at my whiteboard, writing the key words of the Moon, when I had a flash of insight that stopped my world. What if the Moon was more than our inner emotional feelings, our relationship to mother and early habitual childhood responses What if the Moon was so much more? What if the Moon symbolized another part of ourselves that needed my attention? What if we could access that very real part of ourselves? What could that do to heal old emotional beliefs and patterns?

That moment in time began my personal journey into understanding the emotional personality of my inner child.

This is what I learned: The inner child is a container of our emotions. Most people have moments throughout their lives when they're not feeling good about themselves. They feel depressed or angry, acting in ways that they feel are "not themselves." They overeat or drink too much because they want to numb their feelings. When that occurs, their inner child, who contains many of their feelings, becomes numb too.

Exploring our emotions can assist us in discovering our inner children. Take my 3-day challenge. Each day, I would like you to commit to paying close attention to your body and its emotions. Five times a day, stop whatever you are doing, and go inside your body and ask: "What am I feeling right now—mad, glad, sad, scared, or ashamed?" Pay attention to your body's reactions, and you will learn how to determine the emotion and learn more about your inner child's emotional personality. Make sure that you journal your feelings.

The Value of Emotions

Many people think emotions are bad or weak, but I disagree. Many of us are scared that if we feel our feelings to their depths, we'll explode. We create depression instead, stuff our feelings, distract ourselves, and get stuck. In my opinion, feeling is better. I cannot count the number of clients who have heard Michael and me say that feelings trump intellect every time. You will recall my referencing Spangler's seven laws of creating positive energy in your life. His words continually remind me that intellect will never create the goals of my life without my understanding my emotions. Emotions are what give meaning to our lives. They are there to give us the music of our experiences—to show and remind us that a current situation in our life is of value. They are there so we can process it: See the feeling as music, know that what's going on is important, and then figure out a way to handle it. We can feel things, and then we can make choices. Rationality is the ability to use our emotions and intellect together to help us make choices about how we want to handle things. There is nothing we feel that is not God given. Our feelings are sacred, and they actually last a very short time; they come and go. Beginning to appreciate that all of our emotions are valuable to our experiences helps us to open up and to honor and celebrate our feelings—and our inner child contains all of this. Imagine!

Michael and I also divided emotions into two types: contaminated and natural. Clearly, contaminated emotions can create issues in our daily lives: depression, relationship problems, eating disorders, and so on. Our inner children contain our old and, therefore, contaminated emotions. Natural emotions occur in real time and tend to be released quickly.

The Astrological Moon

As I have written previously, the Moon was instrumental in providing me the actual personality of my inner child. This astrological position represents our emotional life, which is built on instincts, moods, feelings, and early mothering. It represents how we wish to be nurtured and how we want our emotional needs met. I kept looking at it, knowing that the Moon represents our emotions, our moods, how we respond to our feelings, and I'd think, "I wonder what that means, really." I was pondering that when, suddenly, it occurred to me that my Moon energy feels very much like the way I felt as a little girl at age 3 after I was raped. With that, I also realized that the Moon shows us the probable nature of our earliest imprints that create what I call our unique inner child.

My astrological chart gave me the answers that I needed to be a good mother and a good father to my inner child, Lynnie. I know what she really needed from her mother and father, because they are clearly delineated in my astrological chart. How often have we heard new parents say, "I wish I had a guidebook for this child!" We do have that guide. It is their astrological chart. One of the first things you will notice is that our inner child usually requires different energies from each parent. Often, they are oppositional. The Moon represents the mother, and Saturn represents the father. Understanding the difference between the Moon and Saturn is vital in being a good mother and father. It is a bit daunting to take on such different roles. Our inner mother and father can help when we get stuck. You will meet them now and learn how to use that information to strategize a positive relationship with your inner child. The challenges are that sometimes we actually get energies that are the opposite of what the charts imply that we need. I will discuss this more later. The situations and experiences that created these feelings occurred many years ago and need to be processed as such. Traumas in your early lives can create inner children that become fixated, or stuck, on the emotions that derived from those experiences. Needless to say, this can create issues in your daily lives: relationship problems, eating disorders, and so forth. As I stated earlier, there are five basic emotions: mad, glad, sad, scared, and ashamed. Emotions are located in your body, and early experiences that may still be unresolved can cause constant trouble with contamination. Your inner child feels these feelings as much now as they did then.

    The Moon gives you valuable information regarding deep emotional patterns imprinted early in your life. It represents how you wish to be nurtured and how you want your emotional needs to be met. The Moon in a chart uncovers your inner child's feelings, sensitivities, and needs around love, nurturing, and being emotionally supported. I started checking in with other people, asking questions of my clients, and invariably I found that the young part of my clients would show up around their Moon sign. I would try to describe to them the child they were at age 3 or 4, and they would say, "That's right, how did you know that?" again and again. That's how I started to really see that there was a connection between our early childhood and the Moon.

I have a little inner child with a Moon in Pisces who was raised in a Southern Baptist home. She was taught to give more than she received. She learned early on that other people's needs were more important than her own. She began volunteering in a state institution for the mentally handicapped when she was 9 years old. Her friends had physical disabilities or were mentally challenged. She loved to take care of them and spent many hours with them. It was what Jesus wanted her to do. My Moon in Pisces was very apparent throughout the 30 years I worked there. She was applauded for acts of sacrifice and chided when she appeared too selfish. Her early childhood foundations were steeped in a philosophy that good things happen to good people when they love Jesus. That was her emotional declaration!

One day, my little girl was very disappointed when people were not responding to my e-mails concerning a workshop and class that I was organizing. She was angry and sad, and she felt that we (my adult self and her) were being treated unfairly. The feelings escalated into tears and then into declarations that Jesus did not love us and that we must be doing something wrong for all of these bad things to happen. My inner child contains my old emotional Pisces beliefs. Her responses to a trivial event came from old, contaminated beliefs. To her, good things should be happening if we do them "RIGHT." My challenge is to help that young, emotionally vulnerable side of me learn that she does not have to worry about being right all the time. I am teaching her that Jesus loves her unconditionally.

As an astrological coach, I have relied on the Moon sign in an astrological chart to give me valuable information concerning my clients' inner child's personality. The Moon also shows us the probable nature of our earliest imprints that create our unique inner child. Next to the Sun, the Moon is the most personal of the Lights. It is the closest Light to us and directly affects the water cycles on Earth (e.g., tides, fish, and the water element in us). Think of some of the phrases we use: "Making waves," "still waters run deep," and "a wellspring of emotions" all water related. The Moon's actions create fluctuation and changes. It moves through the constellations very quickly: one sign in 2.5 days. Because it affects the water element in us, it explains how emotions can change in a short period of time.

The Moon in an astrological chart symbolizes the female principle, the goddess, fertility, the archetypal mother, our unconscious experience, and the inner child. Its glyph is the Moon in the first quarter. The Moon's sign represents familiar patterns from our past that manifest automatically: a mode of feeling and being that occurs spontaneously and automatically. It symbolizes what we need to feel internally secure and "at home with ourselves." Our Moon sign and its experiences feed our deep inner need that provides emotional stability to our personality. The element also symbolizes an important need that our inner child has to have to be secure and safe. Paradoxically, it sometimes tells us what we need to be within ourselves and what our external mother failed to provide.

Understanding the Moon sign in your astrological chart helps you to know and support your little inner child. Please locate your Moon sign from your astrological chart and check the Addendum for its sign and glyph or the astrological legend in your packet to find the English version and write it here: _____. Find your astrological description, and write your personal response in the space provided.

For My Male Readers

Astrologically, men tend to project their Moon sign onto their female partners. That means that you may relate to the challenging aspects of your Moon sign as I describe in this chapter. Your inner child may experience and contain the following energies. Women in your life, beginning with your mother, are there to remind you of old karmic experiences that need to be resolved in this life. You may end up with the "mommy-baby" dilemma: either a mommy looking for a child to take care of or a child looking for a mommy to take care of them. Often, either role is interchangeable and unconscious to the players and evident to others. Within a relationship, you may look for and "hook" a partner who allows you to play mother (taking care of them and protecting them from the outside world) or play baby (someone who will nurture and shelter you). When you project your Moon, you often are unconscious of your tremendous need to mother or be mothered, so you attract partners who are often helpless and orphaned in society. If you are unconscious of the emotional weight of your Moon, partners may play out the emotional energy you desire for yourselves. The Moon needs to complete the parental (mother) image and own its emotional power. Often, the relationship with mother is carried on with the partner (unconsciously, of course). You must learn objectivity within the relationship and must become aware of overdoing sensitivity and empathy. Equality in caring and nurturing works. Learning self-care and self-nurturing needs to be brought into perspective. Resolving mothering issues and karmic relationship issues with mother is vital in the owning of Moon projections. Through this process, you will become your own good mother to your inner child.

Moon in Aries

Your inner child has a Moon in Aries. They are confident, self-aware, physical, athletic, independent and courageous. They need new experiences and are easily bored without them. They see life as an adventure and attack it with enthusiasm and optimism. They need to be offered opportunities to compete with themselves. Their emotional security is often based on their ability to be independent and self-assertive. If they are frustrated, they are quick to anger and can be aggressive in their reactions. They need to learn how to deal with their volatile anger privately so that they can later discuss it more rationally with others. Your Moon in Aries child needs to be taught patience and relational skills. They feel a deep, inner desire to be connected to body movement and physical action. They feel happy and enthusiastic when they are in competition with themselves to be physically fit and strong. Their inner safety and security come from feeling at home with their body. They are the most emotionally secure when they are able to live life as a new adventure.

    Your Moon is ruled by Fire. Fire creates a desire for movement and action. When your inner child deals with new situations, the need for physical activity becomes prevalent. If they are unable to exercise and move their body, they then feel angry or sad. It is difficult for them to wait for things to happen. They want it to be solved right now. They are often ruled by their emotional desires without regard for how others are handling them. They have a strong, independent streak, putting themselves out in the world and usually making an impression.

Comforting Relationship with Mother

Your mother may have been a physically active woman who supported your desire to be strong and competitive. She inspired you to take risks and create new, exciting beginnings. She loved new adventures and took you on them, exploring new, challenging vistas. She understood your need to be angry and allowed you to explore those feelings. She knew you were easily bored, so she created opportunities to challenge you. She admired your natural independence and gave you ways to manifest it.

Challenging Relationship with Mother

You may have had a conflictual relationship with your mother if she did not approve of your basic independent and assertive nature. She might have wanted you to be more considerate and interested in other people's needs and desires. She probably did not approve of your need to be expressively angry. She could have been frightened when you were impulsive and took too many risks.

Your Response

Moon in Taurus

Your Moon in Taurus child is slow to respond to their life experiences. They need to maintain a sense of stability to have the inner security and peace that they require. They do not like change; it feels threatening to them. Often, they can be stubborn and resistant, which is often seen as laziness. These children need to learn that they are intrinsically valuable and that their worth is based not in what they do but in who they are. They are deeply connected to the Earth and need to cultivate this natural ability. Your Moon in Taurus child learns by incorporating their senses, especially touch and smell. They need physical connection, which is why they can be possessive of material items. They are patient, hardworking, and eager to finish their projects. They love the good, comfortable things in life. The world of the five senses is all important to them, as they feel rooted in their ways. They revel in material comforts: Building a solid, comfortable home and foundation helps to keep them feeling safe and content. They are practical and interested in protecting themselves and their own interests. They need to determine whether something is safe and whether there is something of value for them. There is a serenity to them that is calming. It takes a lot to upset them, unless their stability is interrupted. They are not the most adaptable people when that occurs.

Your Moon in Taurus child needs to learn that they are intrinsically valuable and that their worth is based not in what they do but who they are. They need to connect with the Earth through their physical senses. They are often stubborn when confronted. They intrinsically understand the sacred nature of the Earth's elements and know that the Spirit manifests through nature. They are young pantheists seeing the divine in nature.

Comforting Relationship with Mother

Your mother aligned with your desires to have physical

comforts and a stable environment to feel stable and safe. She teaches you the importance of nature and shares her philosophy that God is in all living things. She may even be a gardener showing you her tricks to make things grow. She honored your creative talents. She was a patient woman who was understanding of your bias to move slowly. She provides opportunities for you to have self-worth and self-value.

Challenging Relationship with Mother

Your mother may have disrupted your safety and stability in some way. That would interfere with your ability to trust her. She may have been a fearful and insecure woman and projected those attitudes unto you. She might have a bias to get stuck in old patterns, which could include hoarding. She did not support your innate sense of value, only honoring what you did that was materially successful.

Your Response

Moon in Gemini

Your Moon in Gemini child filters and understands their world through their desire to communication with it. They need to interact with many people to satisfy their curiosity and utilize their minds. They are hurt when they are silenced and not heard. They nurture themselves when they are able to gather information from their world. They hunger for knowledge, and it is important to develop their capacity as thinkers and communicators. These children, when their real needs are not met, can become distracted, lose focus, and communicate erratically and superficially. They prefer to perceive life through their intellectual channels and tend to not deal with their emotions. Your Moon in Gemini child needs to understand that emotions are always present in their bodies. Learning how to communicate with their emotions is a way for them to integrate the need to deal with emotions with their cerebral nature. They nurture themselves when they are able to gather information from their world.

They hunger for knowledge and feel that it is important to develop their capacity as thinkers and communicators. They are usually pleasant, witty, and charming people. They need to interact with many people to satisfy their curiosity and utilize their mind. If gathering information and communication are not available, they may experience nervousness and worry. They prefer to perceive life through their intellectual filter and tend to not deal with their emotions. They often say "I think I feel," which keeps them from dealing with their body, where their emotions live. They seem comfortable with their emotions because they talk about them so easily. However, they do not feel them in their body. When challenged, they would always prefer talking about them and not revealing how they feel. Their tendency to analyze can give them the appearance of emotional detachment. They are versatile and adaptable and need much stimulation from others. They read, talk, and think a lot.

Comforting Relationship with Mother

Your mother could have been well read and intellectual. She was articulate and taught you the power of words and the love of reading. She fostered in you the need to and the and the ability to communicate with all people. She was curious about many things and instilled that in you. Your need to diversify came from her. She fostered a need for you to gather information and share it with others. She taught you to honor living in the gift of presence.

Challenging Relationship with Mother

Your relationship with your mother may be confusing and conflicted. She may have been intellectually strong and emotionally unavailable. She might have been moody and unpredictable. One day, she could be your best friend and, tomorrow, totally detached and remote. She could have been anxious and worried all the time. She futurized by being more concerned about future events and not being able to enjoy living in the present.

Your Response

Moon in Cancer

Your Moon in Cancer child is emotional and sensitive. They sometimes build thick walls to protect themselves when threatened. They have a natural desire to nurture others, and they need that in return. They perceive their environment through their feelings. Moon in Cancer children respond to the emotional reactions of other people. Their moods can change on the basis of these forces. Their strong emotional memory often colors their present life experiences, so emotions control them much of the time. Your Moon in Cancer child only feels secure when they are emotionally stable and those needs are met. They love home and family to such a degree that they will hoard possessions that have emotional memories for them. They have a strong bond with the need to be nurtured and mothered. If it is missing, they tend to withdraw, brood, and get depressed. They are at home with their emotional life when it is stable. However, their moods may change quickly, on the basis of life experiences.

Often, sad feelings can be generated by memories of abandonment and loss.

Their emotional memories of the past are strong and often contaminated. The Moon in Cancer child might hold onto hurts long after others have moved on. They can also be victims of habit, clinging to things, their home, and people they care for. They seek out security and familiarity in all they do. They look for peace and quiet. That attachment to safety might make you afraid of change. These people can have a hard time compartmentalizing their lives, simply because their emotionality knows no boundaries. Sometimes, as a result, they may act emotionally impulsively. In fact, they may be insecure and even manipulative. They need to learn that their past emotions do not need to contaminate their present lives. Holding on to old memories that have no reality in your present is a behavior that needs to change. Being able to do that releases you from contaminated emotions.

Comforting Relationship with Mother

Your mother was emotionally available to you. She taught you the importance of feelings and how to express them. She created a warm and safe home for you and your family. She taught you about your family's traditions and how to establish them in your own life. She knew how sensitive you were and helped you navigate your responses. She loved to cook and taught you how to prepare family dinners.

Challenging Relationship with Mother

Your mother may have emotionally abandoned you. She could have been a stern taskmaster who wanted you to get tough and be less sensitive. She might have been dismissive of warm hugs and family gatherings. She might have a career that is her priority, leaving you with a plethora of babysitters. You may had wanted a very close emotional relationship with your mother. Her inability to bond with you left you sad and then angry. In rare cases, your mother may have actually left you.

Your Response

Moon in Leo

Your Moon in Leo child is playful, fun, and humorous, with a childlike simplicity that is warm and heart-connected. They are highly intuitive, and they put much energy into being supportive and encouraging toward others. They are vulnerable to needing this energy in return. These children are generous and enthusiastic but are easily wounded if not acknowledged, respected, or loved. They are proud and confident and love dramatic creative outlets. They inherently know how to role-play and can become what others want them to be.

Their emotional life is intense, with a need for heart-centered connections to other people. This is why they can be easily be saddened. They feel as if their heart is breaking. When their pride has been hurt, they can create dramatic scenes and pout. This rarely happens in public, only in places where they feel safe. When Moon in Leo children feel comfortable, they love being the center of attention. They require much love and adoration and care in order to function well in the world. They can be rather lazy at times and a little bossy, too. Generally, though, they have a deep need to treat others fairly and justly. They are very proud, and they are rarely happy to follow orders, because they want to be the leader.

Comforting Relationship with Mother

Your mother could have been an actress, filled with a desire to be creative, playful, and generous. Leadership was important to her, and she shared that with you. She loved playing with you and encouraged you to be creative, too. She was youthful, sometimes feeling more like your friend than your mother. You loved her warmth and generosity and learned about the power of your heart from her energy. Her intuition was strong, and often, she could read your emotions. You felt comforted by that. She adored you and wanted to be adored in return.

Challenging Relationship with Mother

Your mother may have been self-centered, wanting attention from everyone, including you. Her heart center felt closed to you, and this broke your heart. You learned not to be vulnerable and trusting. You wanted to play, and she wanted to go out and enjoy herself. You tried many ways to get her attention, and nothing worked. You wanted her to be proud of your accomplishments. Instead, she made them be about her, and you were ignored. You hated that she had to be the center of attention and made a decision never to want that for yourself.

Your Response

_____

_____

_____

_____

_____

Moon in Virgo

Your Moon in Virgo child responds intellectually and analytically to their life experiences. They want to be the good child. This helps them create a sense of order that enables them to adapt to their world. Without this, they are disoriented and emotionally uncomfortable. They have an inherent need to connect with the Earth, and they need practical experiences to relate to their environment. Your Moon in Virgo enjoys serving others by being helpful. Your self-image and self-worth depend on good external results. You want to do the right thing and believe that you need to be not only good but perfect. Often, you procrastinate out of a fear of doing something wrong. You can become critical and judgmental of yourselves and others. You often analyze and dissect your emotional life through a filter of obligation: "I should feel this," instead of what you really feel. This limits your spontaneity. You feel a deep inner desire to find a sense of order in your environment to feel at home within yourself. Your outer world reflects your desire to have inner structure and a sense of inner control. You respond analytically to all experiences without regard to your emotions. You desire perfection and often dissect your emotions, which can inhibit spontaneity. You forget that feelings can cause physical challenges.

You often dissect your emotional life, because you feel you should perform every task to create the perfect solutions. You prefer a simple life in which you feel efficient and useful. You express this best by helping others in little ways. You feel the happiest when you are handling the small details of everyday life. You will take on other people's tasks and sometimes feel overwhelmed by the stress and pressure these actions create. This causes you to worry obsessively. You are reliable, trustworthy, and practical. Others turn to you for help and advice. Your inner child needs to learn that they are perfect just because they exist, not because of what they do.

Comforting Relationship with Mother

Your mother taught you about the importance of being organized and that order would create freedom in your daily life. She taught you that true perfection was inside of you. She helped temper your natural inclination to do everything right and perfect by teaching you that excellence is truly good enough. She modeled the value of giving service to those in need, as long as you took care of yourself first. She taught you good health habits around nutrition and exercise. She taught you the importance of being logical, systematic, and analytical and to honor your emotions as well. She knew that being truly rational was using both of those filters.

Challenging Relationship with Mother

Your mother probably taught you to do everything right or not at all. Anything less than perfect was not acceptable. She wanted you to rely on your intellect and analytical skills. She dismissed your emotional nature as nonproductive and frivolous. Your mother was probably critical and judgmental when you were less than perfect. Her attention and love may have been conditional and based on your actions, not who you were. She may have been obsessed with health and trained you to be an extremist in matters of self-care. She could have been more interested in doing good works of service than to be connected with you.

Your Response

_____

_____

_____

_____

_____

_____

_____

_____

_____

Moon in Libra

Your Moon in Libra child has a strongly developed sense of fairness and justice. They are thoughtful about their emotional life. They weigh both sides of a situation and think before reacting. Because of that, they often are unable to respond, looking ambivalent and indecisive. Balance and harmony are necessary for them to feel tranquil. They want to be in relationship and often fear being alone. They love beauty and refinement and abhor conflict. They inhibit their emotional spontaneity and often have difficulty in understanding their discordant feelings, especially anger. Your Moon in Libra child feels a deep inner desire to finding balance, which is necessary for your emotional serenity. This drive is so powerful that you might do a lot of compromising. They are sympathetic and concerned for others, enjoy socializing, and revel in a good debate. They are eager to please and to see the other's point of view. They weigh both sides of a situation and think before reacting. They feel secure and at home within themselves when they are involved in close relationships and very uncomfortable being alone for long.

Having a mental rapport with others is especially important to them. They feel sad when they are alone, because they have a strong need for partnership. They feel incomplete without someone to share their life. They are creative, loving to work with color and balance for themselves and your environment. They always seem to have someone with them. They find strength and reinforcement with others. They have a strongly developed sense of fairness and justice and are sad when people are not acting with refinement and decorum. They are often flirtatious and charming.

Comforting Relationship with Mother

Your mother may have taught you about refinement and decorum. You learned about creating beauty and elegance in yourself and in your home. She may have had, and shared with you, an interest in interior design. She taught you to be fair and just in your relationships. She helped you learn that conflict does occur and needs to be handled with compromise and third options. You need to change the early habit that you need to always be charming and never cause conflict. She modeled that the most important relationship you had was with yourself. She taught you to find peace in being alone with your own thoughts and feelings.

Challenging Relationship with Mother

Your mother was interested in beauty and refinement. She wanted everything to look good for others' appreciation and approval. Her mantra might have been "What would the neighbors say?" She may have taught you that being attractive was essential to being accepted. She hated conflict and wanted harmony and balance at all time. Because of this, she was often ambivalent and indecisive, finding it difficult to take a stand. She taught you to maintain a sense of decorum at all times. Anger and conflict were not permitted. She might have believed in peace at any price! She may have believed that being in a relationship was necessary to being safe and secure.

Your Response

Moon in Scorpio

Your Moon in Scorpio child is highly emotional, reacting intensely and passionately. They often have deep, chaotic feelings that they need to probe. They need to know what their wants and desires are and will focus on these attitudes until they comprehend them. They can be extreme and negative, with a bias toward secrecy. They have their own agenda and underlying motives that contribute to their sense of mystery. Trust does not come easily. They might bottle up anger and rage and then have blowouts. Moon in Scorpio children feel nurtured when they are giving or receiving intense emotional energy. They need to learn how to embrace, express, and control their emotional life. They feel a deep inner desire to connect with their intense, passionate emotional nature. They need to become masters of emotion. They are able to see beyond the obvious and understand the unconscious core of another. This ability to "probe" this depth can be either intimidating or magnetic to others.

They need to understand the mysteries of life, death, and transformation, which may manifest themselves on many different levels. Your Moon in Scorpio child radiates strength and knowledge. People are drawn to that combination because of that emotional honesty and power. They feel nurtured when giving and/or receiving intense emotional energy. Their fear of vulnerability and losing control can lead to their creating a barrier of inscrutability. Being protective is their way to observe and determine whether they could trust someone else. They seek out commitment, and, once committed, they can be a most loyal and protective partner. This ability to understand human motivation and nature can be very significant to those who feel the same. Helping your inner child determine their wants and desires will help them learn to trust themselves and others.

Comforting Relationship with Mother

Your mother was magical, believing in symbols and ritual,

nature, and the power of positive thinking. She showed her emotions and was very expressive. She taught you the value of knowing and embracing the depth of your feelings. She was passionate about her life and shared that with you. She instilled in you a desire to create what you wanted. She taught you how to use your emotions to connect with others. She would share her love of mystery. Your mother understood the hidden motivations of the people in her life and taught you about the power of the unconscious. She probably gave you a dream diary that she had been keeping until you were old enough to record your own.

Challenging Relationship with Mother

Your mother could have been controlling and emotionally withholding. She could have had trouble showing her true feelings. She taught you not to trust people with your feelings. She may have had situations in her life that caused her emotional pain. She may have held onto this pain and passed it onto you. She might engage in passive-aggressive behaviors and feel emotionally unpredictable to you. Her intensity may have frightened you. She might have warned you not to want something that you may never have.

Your Response

Moon in Sagittarius

Your Moon in Sagittarius child is expansive, optimistic, enthusiastic, idealistic, and philosophical. unless they are being confined in some way. They are happy when they are looking forward to something—a trip, a play date, a walk in the park. They feel emotionally secure when exploring and traveling and also when they can be outdoors and be free to explore. They honor the truth and intuit lies very easily. They must know the meaning of their lives and spend much time searching for it. They question their life purpose and want the people they associate with to care about that also. They can be blunt and direct to a fault. They are truth seekers and speakers but often do not discriminate their truth from the truth of others, assuming that their truth is the only truth. Luckily, they are tolerant and broad-minded and will listen to other views when confronted. They feel a deep desire to connect with their philosophical nature. They love nature and animals. They need their personal freedom and space.

They are spontaneous and love change. They are likely to take leaps of faith that usually work out. Their quest for experiences and desire to share them makes them great teachers. They are at home within themselves when they are aspiring toward or promoting their ideals and comfortable when they are searching for the truth of the meaning of life. They need activity, so meeting new people, being in the world, and traveling it is vital to their happiness. Being in truth with themselves is their most important value. Being lied to causes them to feel sad and angry. Their sense of freedom is the key to their happiness. Inner children might confuse their truth with the truth of others. They might want to help discriminate the difference.

Comforting Relationship with Mother

Your mother was a philosopher, loving the quest for understanding the meaning of life and the adventure of finding the truth. She instilled in you a love of nature and animals and spent many hours walking with you and pointing out the wonders of them. She needed her quiet time and had moments when she had to have space. She loved to travel, and you always went with her, exploring new cultures and new ideas. She taught you the importance of inner and outer freedom.

Challenging Relationship with Mother

Your mother may have claustrophobia and need space and freedom often to recharge. She may have left home for periods of time when she felt confined by the pressures of home and family. You might have learned that escaping is the only way to resolve a conflict. Your mother may have been pedantic, believing that her truth was the only truth. You could have been left believing that too. Your mother might have been somewhat unemotional, relying on her intuition instead. She might have instilled in you a need to be free at all costs.

Your Response

Moon in Capricorn

Your Moon in Capricorn child is born "old," with an unconscious maturity that belies their years. They have a sense of authority and a need for structure. They tend to take on responsibility at young ages. They are goal directed, with a strong desire for success on many levels. These children do not feel their emotions easily, and when they do, they maintain a strong external façade. They can be negative, pessimistic, and restrictive in their family lives. They want to be respected more than anything else, even by their parents. Somehow, they feel like they are in charge: that they are the parents. They often guard their image to look strong, competent, goal directed, and ambitious. You feel a deep desire to control your responses to your life experiences, cautiously projecting authoritative determined energy to realize your goals. You are an earthy person, with a strong attachment to your physical senses. You have been known to set aside personal concerns to perform your duties.

To feel at home within yourself, you must be on top and be the authority. You require organization and efficient management, and you put a lot of value in all things tangible and real. You keep steady and reliable and come across as a competent person. Being useful and productive are basic needs for you. You consider your emotions weak and not to be shared, which can limit your capacity to nurture and being nurtured. Being respected is your major priority so sharing your emotions does not fit with the image you wish to project. You maintain a certain rigidity around emotions. Emotions are messy to you. Your world of emotions is well managed and handled in an efficient and practical manner.

Comforting Relationship with Mother

Your mother may have been a career woman, balancing that with home and family. She was organized and structured and passed these qualities onto you, too. She was a wise woman who taught you the values of integrity and character.

She wanted you to be personally responsible for your actions. You always felt older than your years, so you took on this role easily. You knew your mother loved you, but she was not emotionally demonstrative. She honored and respected your achievements, wanting you to be ambitious and successful.

Challenging Relationship with Mother

Your mother may not have been the nurturing person in your life. She was more interested in building her career and becoming successful than in nurturing her family. She wanted you to be more like her. The more successful you became, the more she respected you. You learned to repress your natural feelings and be strong. You wanted to be loved by your mother but settled for her admiration. There may have been times when you took on a parental role early on in your life to gain your mother's approval.

Your Response

Moon in Aquarius

Moon in Aquarius children are unique, individualistic, socially aware, and altruistic. They are often unpredictable and eccentric, because they are not interested in being the same as anyone else. They are intellectual and want to figure out different tools to solve emotional and social challenges. They can appear detached and even remote, but inside, they are listening to their own drummer. They are the most emotionally secure when they are exercising innovative ideas with freedom. They are emotionally connected to the global consciousness and value their extended community as much as their family. They feel nurtured when their unique natures are encouraged and acknowledged. They do not act as children. They respond more like socially aware adults. They require emotional independence, which can cause an alienation from their true feelings. They live in their heads, not in their bodies, where emotions live.

    Your Moon in Aquarius inner child feels a deep need

to interact socially to feel uniquely humanistic and future oriented. Your inner child feels at home when you are encouraging others and yourself to have freedom and independence. You feel secure when exercising complete freedom of ideas, self-expression, and innovation. You sometimes feel detached and remote when your inner life becomes more important than your outer life. You may grow up feeling "different." Your desire to be uniquely individualized creates a need for emotional independence that causes alienation from your true feelings and aloofness toward the sensitivity of others. They are lifetime students of human nature, loving to analyze why people do what they do.

Comforting Relationship with Mother

Your mother honored your individuated nature. She reinforced your unique and innovative responses to ordinary situations. She knew the importance of your friends and provided opportunities for you to foster these relationships.

She was probably a humanistic person, volunteering to help others. You learned the importance of service from her. She recognized your desire for freedom and independence. She also knew that this could come at the cost of your emotions. She would encourage you to find the rational approach, which is the integration of feelings and emotions.

Challenging Relationship with Mother

Your mother may have been aloof and detached to maintain her desire to be unique and special. Her desire to be an individuated person could have led her to becoming a rebel. You may have inherited that from her. As an intellectual, she could have been emotionally unavailable. You did not learn about the power of emotions from her. An extreme example could be that she left you and was not present at all. This alienation may have kept you from understanding your true feelings

Your Response

Moon in Pisces

Your Moon in Pisces child is emotionally sensitive, compassionate, and empathetic. They are psychically vulnerable to the emotions of others. Often, their feelings are so powerful that they feel a need to escape to imaginative, tranquil, dreamlike places. They hate unpleasantness and conflict and can be fragile and vague in response to it. The world can become too hurtful for this child, so they need creative outlets and periods of retreat to be at peace. Music and the arts are powerful tools to help this child be at peace. They are spiritual by nature and feel a deep emotional void if not connected to their spiritual center. Moon in Pisces children are small spiritual healers who want to connect with others with love and compassion. Their self-value and worth are often dependent on their service to others. They can adapt and flow with changing situations as long they feel that they are helping. They feel a deep desire to emotionally and empathetically connect to others.

They are vulnerable to their emotions, often taking them on as their own. They feel the world can be too hurtful, and they hate conflict and unpleasantness. They want to retreat into their imagination, which is magical and peaceful. If that does not work, they can become sad, if not depressed. They are able to flow energetically with others as long as they know you are in service to them. They know instinctively when they need a recharge. Because of their gentle and sweet nature, they can be easily manipulated by sob stories. These children can put themselves in anybody's shoes with extreme ease. On the plus side, this endows them with remarkable compassion and love.

Comforting Relationship with Mother

Your mother may have been interested in exploring and understanding spirituality. She was emotionally sensitive and imaginative and helped you find that in yourself. She valued your compassion and reinforced that because she was compassionate herself. She might have been in a service career where she was a role model for you to be interested in the same occupation. She may have been a healer and encouraged your natural talents to be one, too. She may have been very artistic and creative and encouraged that in you.

Challenging Relationship with Mother

Your mother may have been too empathetic, taking on others' emotions as her own. She often felt the need to retreat and escape from reality. You want to learn self-care and how to find peace when you are not taking care of someone else. You need to learn how to distinguish when you are being taken advantage of. You may want to find other forms of retreat rather than escaping challenges. Your mother may have been your first experience with someone who cared about others more than herself.

Inner Moon Worksheet

You know your Moon's astrological sign. You have discovered your inner child's personality. Please follow the worksheet to concretize your experiences.

My Moon sign is:

_____

My inner child's emotional needs were met or not met.

Example: I have a Moon in Pisces. I learned about compassion and love of others less fortunate than I. I did not feel special. I needed a great deal of emotional support, because I felt needy and fragile. Yet I needed to be an adult even when I was young. I loved sweets and was allowed to eat as much as I wanted. Food was my reward for being so selfless. It repressed my emotional desires that were not being met.

_____

_____

_____

_____

_____

_____

_____

_____

_____

My inner child makes him- or herself known by:

Example: My child can feel abandoned and scared. Then she hides away and gets depressed. She gets moody and feels sorry for herself. She wants to eat to make the feelings go away.

_____

_____

_____

_____

_____

_____

_____

_____

_____

_____

My inner child's personality can be described as (please refer to the Moon signs and the Astrological Symbolism section in the Addendum):

Example: My inner child's Piscean personality is compassionate and kind. She loves animals and is afraid of people. She is quiet and shy and wants to be safe in a loving environment. She hates anger and conflict and runs away from it. She wants people to be kind to each other.

I can help my inner child understand their feelings by:

Example: I have a Moon in Pisces. I can help my child understand her feelings by honoring her spiritual, magical nature. She gets sad for other people. I can help her understand that she can help others but she doesn't have to feel their feelings. She often feels ashamed if she is not "good." I can give her permission to forgive herself. She is scared that people will judge her. I can help her feel happy within herself.

Your Response

Michael's Story

In 1985, I (Michael) was working part time in psychiatry as a psychotherapist and part time at home as a past-life regressionist/holistic coach. Linda was tuning into wounded inner child work and started to talk to me about it. When I began to tune into this with her, I held it as an interesting and useful "construct," like the psychological constructs I studied in school. I conceived of my inner little boy as a creation of my imagination in my own unconscious mind. I thought of this as a useful way to tap into inner emotions from childhood and a useful way to separate unresolved emotions from childhood from my current emotions as an adult. I continued on this way for a few years as I developed my little boy and my relationship with him. Brother, was I wrong!

When I was a 6-year-old, my birth mother, Lorrain, died of pneumonia on my birthday. That is right, on my birthday! She was in one hospital in Baltimore, Maryland, and I was in another hospital. My mom had chronic lung problems and was in and out of the hospital several times during the last year or so of her life. My Aunt Mary took care of me and my brother for days to weeks at a time in my fifth year. We would go live with her, my uncle, and my unmarried Aunt Helen at my grandparents' house. When my mom died, my family managed to have a funeral and burial while I was still in the hospital. I came home the day after the funeral. There was nothing different to tell me that something had happened. I have no memory of anyone telling me of her death before I came home to my Aunt Mary's house. In fact, I was home for 2 or 3 days before I found out that Mom had "gone to heaven." I have no memory of my older brother saying anything to me about Mom dying, then or ever. I have no memory of Dad ever saying anything to me, either. I do have a direct memory of Aunt Mary telling me of her passing.

    My brother was 3 years older than me, so he would go off to school while I was left in the care of Aunt Mary;

just me and her in the house. I remember being with her for several days when she was sad or quiet or weepy. She would often tear up or cry whenever she was interacting with me. I was confused on those days. My radar told me not to ask why she was crying. I remember and believe that, on the third day, this happened.

Aunt Mary was sitting at the kitchen table doing something—I think she was darning socks. I came up to her and asked for a glass of milk. She turned to look at me and teared up. She held my gaze and spoke to me with her eyes. They said, "I am about to tell you something, and you cannot react. If you do, I will lose it." She then proceeded to tell me that Mom had gone to heaven. I asked if that meant that she was not coming home. She said yes. I said "Oh, okay." Then I asked, "Can I have a glass of milk?" and we moved on with the day. I did not cry that day. I did not cry the next day or the next, or the next. In fact, I did not cry until I was going to sleep one night when I was 11 years old!

That night, when I was 11, I began to grieve my mother's death. I had been holding my breath, so to speak, all those years. My mom was my safe harbor when I was young. She was always there when I needed her. I now know that my dad came back from World War II with posttraumatic stress syndrome. When I was a little boy, my dad could be irritated by things I did that were normal exploratory behaviors for a child. One day when I was around 4 years old, I reached for an ashtray that he was using, and he came at me, angry and loud. He scared me. My mom was entering the room at the time. I remember backing into her protective embrace as she reminded my father that I was just a little boy. So, my dad was not a safe harbor. My brother was not a protective older brother. When Mom died, I was effectively left to be raised by the wolves whom I called family.

Yeah, they took care of me—but I had to watch that I did not get bitten in the butt at the same time. In psychological terms, at 6 years old, I began to repress all my emotions and was stuck in unresolvable grief...for years. That night, as an 11-year-old, I cried alone. I now know that grieving is meant to be a shared process. That is, crying with at least one other human being is required for a heart to heal from the pain of losing someone. I was 23 years old before I cried with someone over my mom dying. My little boy inside was lonely and isolated, and he felt like he did something wrong. He felt like something was wrong with him, but he did not know what. This was, in fact, what caused me to be interested in psychology when I started college.

When I was 9 years old, my dad remarried. My stepmother, Rose, served as my mom as I grew up. I accepted her without any emotional resistance. Rose was a well-intentioned person and nervous most of the time. She was not able to be a safe harbor as my mom was. One day, when I was 15 years old, she showed me a photo album containing a few pictures of my mom. I picked one out to keep. It showed me sitting on my mom's lap at Christmas when I was 5 years old. I was wearing a Davy Crockett outfit (with the sleeves and pants legs rolled up for growing room!). I had a coonskin cap on and was holding a half-eaten candy cane. I was smiling from ear to ear. My mom looked worn out and older than her years, but she was smiling also. Even my dad looked happy in the picture. This was just 3 months before her death; my birthday is March 16. I carried that picture around in my wallet until I was 19 years old.

At 19, I was in the Navy, preparing for active duty in Vietnam. While in a huge boat storage building, I lost my wallet in a boat that my class was working on. I was convinced that someone in my class had found it, removed my meager money, and thrown it somewhere in the hanger or outside in a large field. My class instructor even lined everyone up and offered no recriminations if the wallet showed up by the end of the day without the money. Well, that did not happen. I remember standing outside the hanger that day, looking at the field and thinking that my most valued picture was out there somewhere. I was heartbroken. When I was 29 years old, that wallet (minus any money) came back to me in pristine condition. Some new sailor taking the same class in the same boat hangar 10 years later found my wallet in a compartment on a stored boat in the Naval Shipyard! He then took the initiative to go to personnel and get them to track me down, and he personally mailed the wallet back to me. I considered that an extraordinarily good deed. The Christmas picture with my mom was intact, in pristine condition, in that wallet! I had it laminated and carried that picture in my wallet for another 10 years. At that point, the image had faded so much as to be barely discernable.

    I had dreams of my mom while I was growing up. I had her come to mind at certain times when I was distraught. I would talk to her at times like we pray to God. I had a sense of her presence off and on until my late 30s. Even though she was physically absent from my life, I felt her presence and protection while I was growing up and into my 30s.

In 1985, I started to construct my inner child, Mikey. I saw him as that 5-year-old in the picture with Mom. I began to call him up in my mind each day and give him a hug in the morning. I told him he was a good boy and that I loved him. I would hold and rub and pat until I could feel my heart and his heart relax. This would lead to a safe, warm, loved feeling.

I created a place in my unconscious mind that I call the Sanctuary, or the garden. There is a door in my mind. On the other side of that door is a magical world where you can swim in the land and walk on the water. You can fly through the air or instantly transport yourself from place to place. Here in the garden, manifestation is instantaneous. If you wish for something, it appears. Hand in hand, I created the perfect world for Mikey when I am away in this world, taking care of grown-up business. In this place, he is reunited with his mom. He is reunited with his dad, who is not damaged by the war anymore. Mikey has a dog he loves and a treehouse to live in. He is healthy and free to run and play all day. Mikey is happy and safe and feels loved all the time. He feels parented by me now. He feels unconditional love from me, and I am both good father and good mother to him. His heart is not broken anymore. Because of this relationship I have with him, I can be open hearted and trusting in ways that were difficult for me earlier in my life.

I only began to learn to ski when I was 36 years old (in 1988). Somewhere in those early years of skiing, something amazing happened. One day, I was skiing down a slope that was deserted, except for me. It was early in the day. The snow conditions were perfect. I was going fast and feeling in control without any fear. Suddenly, I heard someone behind me scream, "YAHOO!" You hear that kind of thing around you every so often when you ski. Some people cannot help themselves. I am not one of those people. This "YAHOO!" was so big, that I slowed down and glanced back to see who had yelled. The entire slope above and below me was empty. I looked around in the tree line and groves. I saw no one. Suddenly, I realized that the yell, that sound, had come out of me! As I continued downhill, I felt the separation between myself and Mikey inside. I realized that Mikey had yelled. Mikey was experiencing the pure joy of flying down the mountain on a pair of skis. I was tagging along with my inner child's joy. I could feel joy in him and the joy in me. That was the beginning of Mikey being more than a psychological construct. That was the beginning of realizing that he had been there. I HAD DISCOVERED HIM. I DID NOT MAKE HIM UP. Today, my relationship with Mikey is as real as my relationship with my wife or my biological son.

Michael's Story, Part 2:

I have come to believe that the new body we get with each incarnation has a time when we are free of the karma we bring in from past lives. This time can vary from when we are still in the womb to the first few years after we are born. I have drawn this conclusion from all the past-life work and in-womb regressions I have done over the years. I have observed that our wounded inner child is born from experience(s) we go through in primary childhood, up to the age of 7 years old. The birth of most inner wounded children falls between the ages of 3 and 6 years old.

During the free space, before this happens, we are connected to our body and emotions the way God or providence intended for us to experience life here on the material plane. In modern life, we spend most of our awake time centered in our head. People in natural tribal groups the world over spend most of their awake time centered in their hearts or heart chakras. Before the wounded child is born in us, we are heart centered and, as a result, connected to and aware of our emotions. Our natural connection to our emotions is such that our emotions are not contaminated.

Feeling glad, mad, sad, scared, and ashamed are designed to be reactions to what is occurring right here and right now. In this context, they are designed to enhance our adaptive response to life circumstances and instill meaning to our life experiences. A life lived without emotion is meaningless, regardless of what we do with it.

In modern culture, by the time we reach the age of reason (7 years old), we have learned to live in our heads and be out of touch with our hearts and emotions most of the time. Both cultural training and early emotional trauma leave us cut off from our feelings. When we do connect with our feelings, they are toxic. They are old, unresolved feelings from the past that we ruminate on, or they are toxic feelings generated by anticipating possible future scenarios that may never occur. Past toxic feelings include the unresolved emotions that we bring in from past lives as well. When our inner wounded child is created by some in-life experience, these karmic feelings awaken.

I lived a karma-free childhood until around 3 years old. I do not remember any traumas or unhappy times before then. The early pictures of me then all look clear and happy. "Mikey" was originally created by an event that happened when I was 3 years old. My dad was going out on errands on a sunny spring day. He told my mother, "I'll take Mikey with me." She was surprised and pleased. My older brother was away at school, so she would have a few hours of free time.

    I remember standing on the bench car seat next to my father as he drove to various places: the bank, the post office, and, ultimately, an Esso gas station. Along the way, he bought me a Baby Ruth—my favorite candy bar for years. When we arrived at the gas station, he parked his car and took me into the office with him. There, he began to talk to the owner, Will. Apparently, my dad worked there part time. I remember my dad and Will being familiar and very friendly with each other. While they talked, my dad bought me a 6-oz. Coke from the soda machine. He popped the cap off with the bottle opener and handed the bottle to me. Then, he picked me up and stood me on top of Will's desk.

He asked Will about getting some new tires for his car. Will replied, "Well, let's go in back and look at what we have." My father told me, "Stay here, I'll be right back." Then, he and Will walked out of the office into the bays and turned out of sight. He left me standing on the desk, holding the Coke bottle with both hands. I remember that this all happened amazingly fast. When he disappeared from my sight, I became terrified. At the same time, a strange man walked into the office. He looked at me, smiled broadly, and said, "You must be John's boy." I had a panic reaction. The next thing I remember, I woke up in a hospital!

Here is what happened: When the strange man approached me, I had a grand mal seizure and blacked out! He managed to catch me before I fell onto the concrete floor. I don't know what happened to the Coke bottle. My father rushed me to a nearby hospital. It happened to be the one where I was born. Ironic, huh? An EEG revealed epileptic-like patterns in my brain waves. I was placed on phenobarbital until I was 11 years old and a follow-up EEG showed no signs of epilepsy. I am not epileptic in this life. That was the day my karma kicked in. As I moved forward, FEAR was always with me. I was scared all the time in my gut. It got big. It got small. It was never completely gone; that is, except when I was being tactilely comforted by my mom.

Three years later, on my sixth birthday, my mom died. Aunt Mary discloses this to me in such a way that I shut down and suppress my grief. Fear and sadness dominate my growing-up years. Mikey is the one who holds all this for me as I develop into an adult. I only begin to reconnect to my emotions when I start college and begin studying psychology.

Fast forward to 1985, when I began the exercise of constructing my inner child, Mikey. At the time, we had a collie named Tara. While I was forming an emotional relationship with Mikey, Tara was forming a heart-centered relationship with me. Tara would come to where I was sitting, and she would jump up and place her paws on my shoulders. Her heart would be on top of my heart. She would literally hug me. Then, Tara began to sit facing me, staring up at me. She would do this over and over until I got down on my knees and hugged her. While I was learning to hug Mikey on the inside, Tara was teaching me about the value of hugging on the outside. Dogs are utterly amazing! I think Tara felt the presence of Mikey inside me.

Today, I feel emotionally clear underneath. It took years to crest that mountain inside. It took until my early 50s to be able to live in the here and now most of the time. It took that long to fully connect with my heart center and live there most of the time. I could not have done it without Mikey. That is how it works. I, the adult, began by trying to save and heal the wounded child, and, at some point, the inner child ended up saving me. Mikey is the part of me that keeps me connected to my empathy. Mikey shows me how to be creative, have fun, play, love life, and be optimistic. That is my story…and I am sticking to it!

SATURN AND YOUR INNER FATHER

Your Saturn

Saturn in your astrological chart is the energy of your inner father as well as indicative of your actual birth father. It represents your teacher providing information on your needs for security and safety through tangible and earthy achievement. It defines the discipline, effort, and reliability that will become the foundations of your character and integrity. Its limitations teach maturity through patience, endurance, and humility. Often, your Saturn placement tells you the kind of father you wished you had. It then creates obstacles/delays and difficulties/hardships that you need to overcome to become a wise, spiritual adult. Its symbolic heat and pressure are needed for you to develop your fundamental nature. By showing us the value of work and effort applied to our daily lives, it continues to bring us face to face with the reality of the material world. It is also your karmic teacher, bringing forth unresolved obligations and conflicts from other times.

These challenges may manifest in your choice of father in your current life. Paradoxically, it sometimes tells us what we need to be within ourselves and what our external father failed to provide. Understanding your Saturn sign in your astrological chart helps you to know and support your little inner child. Please locate your Saturn by its sign and glyph. Write it here: _____. Find your astrological description, and write your personal response in the space provided.

For My Female Readers

Astrologically, women tend to project their Saturn sign onto their male partners. That means that you may relate to the challenging aspects of your Saturn sign as I describe in this chapter. Your inner child may experience and contain the following energies. Saturn is the father figure, the conditional parent, so when you project Saturn onto a partner, you may be entering a father–child situation. If you deny your Saturn, you may have a partner who seems authoritative, limiting, cold, and overly responsible. You may feel restricted by your partner and blame him for being too rigid and inflexible. However, you must first ask yourselves what it is within yourself that reacts so strongly to this authoritative partner. Perhaps there is unfinished business with your own perception of father. Power is also an issue here, as well as work. Both can be overdone.

When Saturn is projected, the power of the partner's control may seem threatening or limiting. Saturn also represents the Shadow—that part of yourself that you constantly disown. The Shadow is that part that you usually are acting from when you exclaim, "Oh, that wasn't me," or "Usually, I am not like that." The conscious ego tends to deny these characteristics. When you project your Saturn onto your partner, often there is blame attached to the partner's behavior that reminds you (unconsciously) of your own Shadow. Saturn is responsibility and demands that you take charge of your Shadow side in the relationship. Through this process, you will be able to become a good father to your inner child.

Locate your Saturn placement in your astrological chart and find the English version by its sign and glyph in the Addendum. Write it here: _____. Then, among the following descriptions, find the one that matches yours and write it in the space provided.

Saturn in Aries

Your Saturn in Aries helps you create the goals, order, and structure in your life to become a responsible, thoughtful, independent, spiritual adult. Saturn presents the real- life challenges necessary to becoming a person who takes actions. This encourages self-awareness, self-confidence, and self-motivation. Your Arian nature wants you to take thoughtful risks, spring into action, and take personal stands when necessary. Your Saturn in Aries stimulates you to have the strength of will to become more self-assertive and to take more initiatives when appropriate. You are responsible for creating new beginnings to explore and new adventures to experience. You need the discipline necessary to having a strong, physically fit body. You are competitive with a desire to be first and win.

You have learned that self-respect is of utmost importance to you. You have learned that being self-aware is vital to your accomplishing your goals. You are responsible to modeling self-assurance and self-confidence, which is inherent in all people you encounter. You want them to embrace it as you have learned to. You are totally self-reliant. You do not want to be told what to do. You are ambitious when it relates to creating new experiences. If your goal is to climb a mountain, you will achieve that by being persistent and super focused.

Comforting Relationship with Father

Your father valued physical accomplishments. He taught you the importance of physical fitness. He may be a strong spiritual warrior who coaches you to be the best you can be. He wants you to have the self-awareness to be a good leader without being concerned if you are followed. He wants you to stand your ground and be strong in your beliefs. He might caution you to take risks that are well thought out. He might want you to become a first responder, a sportsperson, or a warrior.

Challenging Relationship with Father

Your father could be a man whose career has a certain amount of danger associated with it. You may have seen him get into problems because of it. That might have caused you to avoid involving yourself in anything that seems dangerous. If your father was a risk-taker, you may be afraid of that. You could have had a father who was not present in your life, causing you to become overly responsible as a child. Your father might have taught you to be overly ambitious and competitive and that winning was everything.

Your Response

_____

_____

_____

_____

_____

_____

Saturn in Taurus

Your Saturn in Taurus helps you create the goals, order, and structure in your life to desire a secure and serene life. Your love of the Earth, manifested through the practical realities of cooking and creating usable art such as pottery, is inspired by your father. You could have a need to create successful methods of handling financial matters in the banking and investment fields, as well as in real estate. It will provide you the wisdom to create a firm "earthy," foundation built with patience and determination. Building a home, honoring the land, and having comfort are significant elements to fostering your inner peace. You know that being personally responsible will bring you the material success necessary to having secure foundations. You have the wisdom to know that inner self-value is critical to that external success. You are committed to obtaining success on every level. Success for you is the integration of spiritual values and material success. Ownership of the land is a symbol of your patience and determination as you watch plants grow. Making money through earthy endeavors is critical to your need for security.

Comforting Relationship with Father

Your father is a strong, patient, determined presence stimulating your creative talents. He knows that you can transition those talents into material success as you build your earthy foundations. He taught you to honor the Earth and could have been a great chef, an architect, or a gardener. He inspired you to learn how to create good, practical foundations that would provide you safety and security. He may encourage you to integrate material and spiritual values into your daily life. He encourages you to explore and manifest your creative talents to increase your self-esteem and self-value.

Challenging Relationship with Father

Your father could be a man whose material life was challenging. You learned from him the importance of having financial security. He may not have provided you with firm foundations that you know are necessary for your self-esteem. He may be obsessed with making money, which left you feeling ignored and abandoned. He may not have honored your creative nature, wanting you to be more practical to become successful.

Your Response

_____

_____

_____

_____

_____

_____

_____

Saturn in Gemini

Your Saturn in Gemini helps you create the goals, order, and structure in your life needed to become a spiritual messenger. Saturn presents the real-life challenges necessary to becoming a cosmic adult. You must structure and organize a practical and secure intellectual foundation. Your Saturn in Gemini provides you opportunities to gather information. The path to your soul mission is to be intellectually wise, communicating productive ideas to those who need them. As you become responsible in becoming a communication chameleon, you will have the ability to talk to a variety of people with different needs. You need to commit yourself to living in the present and exploring those moments to their fullest. However, you may be interested in information with a focus on exploring the past and its influences on the present. Your sense of discipline leads you to long-term research and creating structures of logic and organization.

    The combination of your logic and ability to

communicate makes you a great debater and provides opportunities for your success in any area involving those components. You know that being personally responsible for your intellectual curiosity and being a messenger of the gods is vital to your path to significance. You are committed to being interested in information exploring the past and its influences on the present.

Comforting Relationship with Father

Your father is bright, curious, and determined. He is probably an information gatherer and taught you to value being the same. His presence provides you the motivation to be the spiritual messenger for all people. He honors your intellectual ability and fosters your innate love of words, information, and the knowledge that is generated from that. He helps you maintain a relationship with the present and a desire to probe the past. Your father wants you to become a strong and versatile communicator to share ideas, thoughts, and philosophies. He encouraged your active listening skills.

Challenging Relationship with Father

Your father could have been a man who judged your intellectual abilities. His facility with language may have threatened and intimidated you, because you could not keep up with him. He may have found you wanting in the areas of communication. He may have criticized your inability to match his success. You may have learned to be afraid of talking to other people for fear of doing it wrong. Your father might be a futurist, not honoring living in the present and, therefore, not teaching its importance to you.

Your Response

_____

_____

_____

_____

_____

Saturn in Cancer

Saturn in Cancer helps you create the goals, order, and structure in your life to become a divine integrated feminine person. It will stimulate you to learn about your emotional life and be able to express your feelings. This learning does not come easy. You would need to become responsible for your emotional awareness and openness. This takes effort to be achieved as you mature. You need to find the strength to be vulnerable and sensitive to others' emotional needs. Your Saturn in Cancer encourages your need to be nurturing, feminine, and more mothering and provides the stability necessary for you to achieve this. It wants you to find ways to alter your old negative beliefs and embrace your inner child. This child needs your nurturing.

You may be drawn to careers connected to food preparation or nurturing. You are drawn to water, so you may choose a career connected with it. Your Saturn in Cancer wants you to commit to creating and building an emotionally secure and happy home environment for your family You would need to become responsible for emotional awareness and openness. This takes effort to be achieved as you mature. You need to find the strength to be vulnerable and sensitive to others' emotional needs. You desire to be nurturing. Your success is predicated on your ability to understand your feelings. You will learn that emotions create the drive to be ambitious and successful.

Comforting Relationship with Father

Your father may feel like an integration of male and female energy. He wants you to be the same: strong, mature, and responsible as well as emotional, sensitive, and compassionate. Your father wants you to find ways to alter any old negative beliefs and become more youthful and childlike. He models what responsibility for being emotionally nurturing looks like. He teaches the value of family traditions and the importance of home.

Conflicting Relationship with Father

You may have had a father who was not able to understand and display emotions. Your childhood may have been more logical and practical, leaving little room for emotions. This would provide opportunities for you to learn to be totally responsible for your emotional awareness and openness. You may not have had a close family environment but yearn for that. Your family may have been disrupted by the loss of your father.

Your Response

_____

_____

_____

_____

_____

_____

_____

_____

Saturn in Leo

Your Saturn in Leo helps you create the goals, order, and structure in your life to become a divine leader. Without it, you could not accomplish your soul's purpose. Saturn presents the real-life challenges necessary to becoming a cosmic adult. It will stimulate your need to learn about inspired leadership. It will teach you to embrace the strength and courage of your heart. Your heart will provide opportunities for you to love, honor, and respect yourself. From self-empowerment, you will become the confident leader and teacher that you need to inspire others. Your Saturn in Leo provides you opportunities to embrace the joyful, spontaneous child within. Learning to have fun with that child will continue to open your heart. Saturn and Leo are at cross-purposes. Saturn does not want to be center stage, and Leo demands it. Your Saturn in Leo will be afraid and defensive about being put into that situation. With maturity, your leadership quality will resolve the conflict, and you will know that it is safe to draw attention to yourself. You need to become a self-confident, courageous, inspired leader to those who seek it from you.

Comforting Relationship with Father

Your father might be an inspired, charismatic leader. He encourages you to be confident, strong, and courageous. He is generous and open-hearted, playful and fun-loving. He often initiates games that your whole family enjoys. He is able to assess his inner child and teaches that to you. He is a person to be respected for his abilities to be in leadership roles and often is the center of attention. You admire him and want to emulate his abilities.

Challenging Relationship with Father

Your father might have been self-centered and self-absorbed. His childishness embarrasses you. He wants to be loved and adored at any cost. He is always eager to be the center of attention. His parenting skills leave much to be desired, for he is the child looking to you for guidance and approval.

Your Response

Saturn in Virgo

Your Saturn in Virgo helps you create the goals, order, and structure in your life to become a practical healer. At its most discriminating, Saturn in Virgo has the need to be responsible for understanding the true meaning of internal not external perfection. However, your expectations and your need for perfect outcomes can bring anxiety or may create health challenges. Your great commitment is to be of service to others, especially in the area of physical and emotional health. You are a practical healer. You serve others by teaching them to have physical and work habits that support their mind, body, and soul. It will stimulate you to create order out of chaos by being organized and efficient. Your mind is very methodical, and putting everything in its own box brings you pleasure.

Thus, organizing data or processes may become, for Saturn in Virgo, a joyful experience. Such people are definitely great in categorizing things or information, putting their own order to anything. Saturn in Virgo teaches you to be highly discriminating, using your analytical and logical strengths. Instead of being overwhelmed by details, incorporate them into a system that encourages productivity. The path to your soul mission is to be a voice of discernment and logic and to encourage health and congruence in yourself and others.

Comforting Relationship with Father

Your father is the supportive part of you that wants to serve others as a better health provider. He teaches you to honor your analytical mind and helps you create good structures to be more organized. He is responsible for helping you understand the true meaning of internal, not external, perfection. He helps you learn the importance of intellectual discrimination.

Challenging Relationship with Father

You may have had a father who was judgmental and critical. He probably did not appreciate your compassionate nature. He may not understand your desire to help other people. He might not honor your career of service. It is possible that he may even feel intimidated by your innate intelligence. He may not be a good role model in the area of order and organization.

Your Response

_____

_____

_____

_____

_____

_____

_____

_____

Saturn in Libra

Your Saturn in Libra helps you create the goals, order, and structure in your life to become a mediator and cosmic judge. Saturn in Libra encourages you to find the true balance and harmony between yourself and others. You may decide to wait before getting too involved in a relationship, preferring a logical rather than an impulsive one. You are often blessed with long-term harmony and balance in your relationships. You are a mediator, sharing ideas that will create negotiation and mediation, putting yourself in another's shoes to foster understanding and communication. Your diplomatic skills are very beneficial when it comes to seeing the gestalt of any important challenge. You want to creative opportunities for you to search for fairness and justice. Balance and harmony are also displayed in your use of color and symmetry to produce beauty and peace in your environment.

Comforting Relationship with Father

Your father believes in creating balance in his life and teaches you those values. He understands the importance of fairness and justice and sets a good example of this for you. He is artistic and loves culture, the arts, and refinement. He wants you to be a person who uses compromise and third options instead of being extreme.in response to life's situations. He loves being in relationships and is excellent at communicating the values and skills necessary to facilitate balance and harmony.

Challenging Relationship with Father

You may have had a father who is indecisive and ambivalent in his relationships. He wants balance and harmony to such a degree that he is unable to take thoughtful actions. He might have been emotionally off balance in ways that caused you pain. His desire to be love and adored could cause him to be flighty and superficial. He may get stuck in beliefs that life is unfair and unjust. He may be too interested in keeping up with the Joneses.

Your Response

Saturn in Scorpio

Your Saturn in Scorpio helps you create the goals, order, and structure in your life to become an emotional transformer. Without it, you could not accomplish your soul's purpose. Saturn presents the real-life challenges necessary to becoming a cosmic adult. You are responsible for turning chaos into intensity and fear into powerful drive. You will be able to pursue success with great determination and vigor. You are relentless in situations to the best of your ability. Saturn in Scorpio helps you reframe your anger and resentment into a passion for more creative pursuits, such as philosophy or emotional and sexual intimacy.

You need to commit yourself to probing the mysteries of life and finding your personal answers to significant questions. The path to your soul mission is to use your desire and will to understand and connect with and help others with their passions. You desire to make partnerships successful and healthy for all concerned. You are relentless in helping others, whether in probing their unconscious or helping them access their emotions.

Comforting Relationship with Father

Your father is an emotionally passionate man who teaches you about ways to use your innate resources to connect with others. He will help you turn chaos into intensity and fear into powerful passion and drive. He will aid you with great determination and vigor to accomplish your goals. He believes in becoming a master of his own emotions. He understands the power of the unconscious and wants to help others discover theirs.

He loves natural magic and rituals and the importance of dream interpretations. He loves sharing all of this with you.

Challenging Relationship with Father

You may have had a father who did not express his emotions, because he does not trust easily. He withheld his emotions from you also. His self-containment and aloof manner may have caused you to feel abandoned. He might have not been financially successful and out of control with money issues. You might have experienced your father as having problems with rage and may have been frightened when he lost control. Your father could have been manipulating and controlling, leaving you feeling angry.

Your Response

_____

_____

_____

_____

_____

_____

_____

Saturn in Sagittarius

Your Saturn in Sagittarius helps you create the goals, order, and structure in your life to become a philosopher. Without it, you could not accomplish your soul's purpose. Saturn presents the real-life challenges necessary to becoming a cosmic adult. It presents opportunities for you to be responsible for structuring your philosophy so it can be shared and taught to others without intruding your truths on them. You explore travel and other cultures and religions to learn more. You commit yourself to organizing your life based on optimism, truth, and personal freedom. You catalyze your penetrating mind to search for depth and meaning in life. You understand your inner spiritual teacher and embrace your inner faith and serenity each day. You believe in the philosophy of serendipity and honor the unexpected surprises it brings.

Comforting Relationship with Father

Your inner father is highly intuitional, with a wealth of spiritual information that he is happy to share with you. He has taught you the philosophy of serendipity and asked you to share the unexpected surprises that it brings. He is optimistic and expansive. He passed on his love of nature and philosophy to you. You took many trips with him, exploring the great outdoors. He loved freedom of thought and action and taught you all he knew. He was optimistic and expansive in his search for life's meaning and truth.

Challenging Relationship with Father

You may have had a father who was rigid in his religious beliefs. He felt that his spiritual truth was the only path and was pedantic and dogmatic. He probably imposed that onto you. He could have been an absentee father, taking many trips away from the family. He could have been claustrophobic, with an obsessive need for freedom. His commitment phobias could extend to his being a parent to you. He had a bias to being negative when you wanted him to teach you about being philosophically optimistic and expansive. Some fathers experience gambling addictions.

Your Response

Saturn in Capricorn

The energy of Saturn in Capricorn helps you be responsible for finding your road to success and for organizing and following it with persistence and determination. Claim your authority and ambition, and patiently climb your personal mountain to achievement. You need to commit yourself to self-discipline, self-responsibility, and self-actualization by deliberately ordering your internal and external life. You understand that self-reliance and self-containment are vehicles to personal responsibility and that integrity and self-honor are the foundations for success. You also have the desire to be successful and the persistence to achieve it.

Saturn in Capricorn augments your wisdom and love through your protection of and loyalty to your family and friends. You want the path to create an ordered, structured, responsible approach to appropriate goals that will manifest as a mature and wise life. You will establish personal traditions that will endure over time, because you honor the past and what it can teach you. Through understanding history as a guide to understanding the future, you will learn more of the history.

Comforting Relationship with Father

Your father is highly motivated and ambitious in helping you become a wise, successful man. He will help you remember enduring family traditions that become your emotional foundations. His love of history will help you honor your past. He will share with you the importance of self-reliance and personal responsibly. He will teach you how to organize and structure your life's commitments and goals. You watch him love and honor you and his family. You feel his respect for you, and that inspires you to be better. Your father encourages you to have the wisdom and self-discipline to climb your personal mountain to success.

Challenging Relationship with Father

You may have had a father who was not interested or unable to be successful. He might have had few goals and little desire to be ambitious. On the other side of the coin, your father could be a severe taskmaster who was emotionally unavailable. He could be more interested in money and status than nurturing his family. You might have had an absent father altogether. He may have been irresponsible in his work and family. This loss may have caused you to fill the vacuum that this has created.

Your Response

_____

_____

_____

_____

_____

_____

_____

Saturn in Aquarius

Your Saturn in Aquarius helps you create the goals, order, and structure in your life to become a mediator. Without it, you could not accomplish your soul's purpose. Saturn presents the real-life challenges necessary to becoming a cosmic adult. With Saturn's help, you have the responsibility to claim your originality and individuality. Find your humanity, and translate it into a political and spiritual cause; then join with others who feel the same way. Understand your rational, logical, and observing nature but also the holistic model (mind, body, and spirit), and integrate it into your approach to life. Maintain an equal, humanistic view in the groups you join and the friends you keep. The path to your soul mission requires that you be avant garde, visionary, and uniquely different in your objectives.

Comforting Relationship with Father

Your father is a man with innovative views. He is interested in technology and science and how they can support humanitarian goals. He demonstrates a strong desire to be a unique individual, wanting to make a difference in his world. He is a leader with strong new-age ideals in supporting others. He is usually a part of a like-minded group that has common goals to help those less fortunate. He understands the Aquarian triangle of mind, body, and soul and how they create integration for healing. Your father is interested in your learning to be a rational person—the integration of intellect and emotion. He supports your benign revolutionary approach to your life situations.

Challenging Relationship with Father

You may have had a father who was detached and emotionally cold. He may be erratic and moody. He may be a rebel against traditional values and attitudes. You may have inherited some of your father's weird and strange behavior. Because of that, you may have rebelled against his behaviors to find your own innovative changes that support your humanistic ideals. You may have learned how to be benignly detached as you are more observant and not reactive.

Your Response

Saturn in Pisces

Your Saturn in Pisces shows you the truth about why you might have challenges to your spiritual beliefs. You have a bias to be emotional and may be a bit vulnerable. You need to commit yourself to using your psychic and intuitional gifts to help others. You want to claim your spiritual and creative talents and to experience life as an imaginative, magical, and spiritual adventure. Your responsibility is to provide gentle service to self and others.

You are compassionate and sensitive to others without giving yourself away. Your Saturn in Pisces wants you to find inner strength, self-sufficiency and the ability to create structures, organizations, and order under your own initiative. You have the potential to develop strong inner discipline and sensitivity. You may experience old feelings of doubt and a lack of confidence in yourself, but this will pass as you continue to develop your faith. Your love of solitude will strengthen you as you need to commit yourself to using your psychic and intuitional gifts to help others claim their spiritual and creative talents.

Comforting Relationship with Father

Your father may be an emotionally strong spiritual healer. He might encourage your own spiritual gifts of empathy and desire to serve. He wants to help you become more emotionally aware. He has taught you have a responsibility for understanding your feelings and expressing them through a strong sense of self. He honors your vulnerability and helps you contain it when it damages you. He may be a sensitive person who loves music and the arts. He may encourage you to find those talents within yourself. He may have created a career of service that you may want to emulate. If you have a bias to becoming a martyr, your father will help you learn how to take care of yourself as well as others.

Challenging Relationship with Father

You may have a father who was very emotionally challenged. He may have masked troublesome feelings with drugs or alcohol. He had a strong female energy that might have felt weak to you. He could have married a strong woman who was dominating and controlling. He may have criticism of your psychic and intuitional gifts to help others. Your desire to claim your spiritual and creative talents and to experience life as an imaginative, magical, and spiritual adventure may feel crazy and irresponsible to your father. Your father may not have demonstrated a strong sense of self-worth and self-esteem, which you may not demonstrate also.

Your Response

_____

_____

_____

_____

Inner Father Worksheet

My inner child was hurt because my father was:

Example: I have Saturn in Gemini. I had two fathers: one who betrayed my mother and left us and a stepfather who was an alcoholic. Neither father supported my innate curiosity and brightness. My stepfather actually told me, "You are a liar and the truth is not in you." I was unable to speak my mind without fear of judgment. I developed a stammer. I would carry that with me for years. I was hurt that I was repressed and denigrated for being smart. I developed a fear of speaking in public.

I can be a responsible inner father to my inner child by:

Example: I have Saturn in Gemini. My good father honors and respects my little girl's innate brightness. He gives her opportunities to say what she wants and finds her cute, funny, and very smart. He answers all of her questions without judgment. He reminds her how important it is to live in the present moment. Because of that, she is much happier.

Challenges to Discovering Your Inner Child

Karen's Challenges

What is my inner child? That has been such a theoretical concept for me. I have spent many sessions with Linda and Michael and uncovered blocks for myself hearing, "This is linked to your inner child." I have walked away stumped and frustrated, wanting to have clarity and understanding. What was this inner child to do for me or within me? What benefit could come from paying attention to something so abstract to finding value for myself?

Honestly, I have been digging at this for a few years now, and the pieces of this puzzle fall very slowly into place for me. Behaviors that have embarrassed me or that I did not like unconsciously came through my inner child. For me, as an extremely logical person, this did not fit: How do I blame an inner child for poor choices or behaviors? Where did this kid sit in me? I could not feel that person/child within me.

What the hell did it really mean? It all felt hypothetical and produced no meaning or feelings within me.

What if I could feel and understand my inner child; what would this gain me? What might I learn from a child, or how might my childlike behavior hold me back?

I have discovered for myself that there are parts of me that I have denied and not nurtured. I was raised to be an adult since early childhood. I was taught that caring for others made me a good girl; that is how I was loved. What skills did I have to care for myself and now this inner child? I only understood this when Linda asked how I had loved and nurtured my own children. Had I been that loving and nurturing to myself? This helped me know that having fun and taking joy in small pleasures nurtures my inner self—the child within me. A larger part for me has ignored and neglected negative beliefs that I held true. This is when the petulant child reacts like a small child with its hands over its ears. I now recognize that this is my inner child coloring my thoughts and feelings in a challenging way. I am slowly unwinding this inner child and am healing my relationship with her on an almost daily basis.

She has been a very strong and cynical part of myself and my unconscious beliefs and behavior patterns. I certainly do not have it all figured out. She and I have so much to learn together. However, I now have the ability to recognize and feel an awareness of these internal, unconscious, childlike behaviors. I know that being heart-centered with her will help me in this lifetime and many more.

STRATEGIES TO HELP YOU DISCOVER YOUR INNER CHILD

The key is understanding who your inner child is and what he or she feels and wants. What we do with our inner children comes after we understand who they are. Remember that the child in you is pure feeling. This isn't a rational exercise but an emotional one. The point of this is to help you deal with your inner child's feelings, but first, you have to know what they are. It requires digging into your childhood. The first thing you need to do is give your child a name that is not your adult name. Pay attention—your inner child will whisper his or her name in your ear. There was a real moment in our lives when we got stuck as the result of a certain experience. That experience becomes the unconscious emotional driver in our life until, or unless, we deal with it.

As children, it is appropriate to want our parents to take care of us. Often, our parents are not aware of what their children really did. We as adults need to do that! Most people

I've worked with have inner children at around 3 or 4 years old. Sometimes they're older, when accidents or situations occur at 6 or 7, resulting in a major trauma. From 0 (birth) to 3 is really where all the emotional imprints occur. At that age, children are responding to situations purely from emotion. From ages 3 to 7, children are becoming more intellectual; they are starting to see some separation between themselves and others. By age 7, they go through the first level of understanding themselves as separate beings. They have more of a sense of their intellectual selves and more of a sense of disconnect from their parents.

In childhood, children receive information and handle their environment emotionally. They have emotional instincts and reactions; they are emotional sponges. They cry when they're hungry or when they fall down, they hit when they get mad, and they jump up and down with excitement when they get a new toy or a treat. They are emotionally driven until they reach the age of reason, which is usually around age 7. In childhood, children receive information and handle their environment emotionally. They have emotional instincts and reactions; they are emotional sponges. They cry when they're hungry or when they fall down, they hit when they get mad, they jump up and down with excitement when they get a new toy or a treat. It's been proven that people who start alcohol or drug addictions in their youth stop growing emotionally. They imprint at the age when they started using, and they get stuck at that developmental level.

However, I am able to recognize and be aware of these internal, unconscious, childlike behaviors. They have to get through that imprint to start growing again, which can be very challenging. The same kind of thing happens in early childhood. We all had some experience that caused an emotional imprint in us at the age when we were the most emotional that we really need to look at and understand. It could have been the birth of another child, a move to a new home, the loss of a parent due to death or even to a new job, or any number of other things. Pay specific attention to the areas of life that you struggle with now, and see if anything they tell you or anything you recall relates to your current situation.

Next, think about your relationship with your parents. There's a bias, especially in the first 3 years of our life, to the mother, unless it's a role-reversal family in which the father becomes more of the nurturing parent than the mother. I'm not ruling that out, but generally speaking, in the first 3 years of life, the mother is the most emotionally nurturing and the most in contact with the child, so the mother has more impact at the early ages. What are your main emotions about your mother? What are your judgments of her? Our mothers don't always give us everything we wanted as children, so it's important to know what you wanted from her that you did not receive. You reviewed this doing your worksheet. Young children want security, attachment, care, and concern. They want love, attention, affection, and connection.

As the child gets older, the father gets more involved. Classically, the father teaches the child about responsibility, integrity, character, structures and systems, how to be in the world professionally and financially, and how to be rational and intelligent. The father is typically more intellectual than emotional. The father plays games, and provides toys, and involves children in sports. Did your father do these kinds of things for you? How do you feel about your father?

Find Early Childhood Pictures

Create a chronology of early childhood pictures. Study these photographs. You are looking for changes in emotions. It is difficult to parent children if you are unaware of them. It is also challenging if you do not know their ages. Old photographs and your imagination really help you to have a clear vision of your inner child. Meditation can take you right to them. It is good to find out their ages. You can go into a meditation, talk about what's going on with them, and ask how old they are.

Start by thinking about your childhood and any major events that happened to you between birth and age 7. Go through childhood photographs to get a sense of your emotions through the pictures. Do you look happy in the pictures? Do you see any shifts in your emotions at a certain age? Look for as much detail as they can give you about the kind of child you were and the important events that happened in your childhood.

The following exercises will help you determine the age of your inner child. You will discover minor shifts that will help you find your inner child's age. Did your parents move when you were young? Did Daddy leave Mommy? Was a brother or sister born? Your history and your photographs provide information about the imprinted age of your inner child. I also know that it works! Many of my clients have taken on the role of being a good parent to their inner children. They have had remarkable successes. They have lost weight, learned to love exercise (after all, most healthy children like to run and play), and have found joy in life's wonderful moments. They understand their emotional lives more deeply. They come from compassion and do not automatically judge or denigrate themselves.

Meet Your Inner Child Meditation

Michael Brady's gentle, guided hypnotic meditation will enable you to experience a visceral, emotional relationship with your inner child. Allow yourself a half hour to be quiet and still, with no external interruptions. Listen to this first meditation and meet your inner wounded child. Journal your experience in the following space. This meditation can be found at KarmicFreedom.com/Store available for purchase to accompany this chapter.

_____

_____

_____

_____

_____

_____

Find Your Baby Book

Many of us have baby books begun by our parents. If you can find it, look at it for benchmarks and events that your parents thought important enough to write down. Journal your information in the following space.

_____

_____

_____

_____

Listen to Your Family's Stories

Write down stories that your family shared with you about your young life. Ask them questions. Do they spark any memories? Journal the information in the following space.

_____

_____

_____

_____

_____

_____

_____

Observe Other Children

Watch children who are about the same age as your inner child. If you have children, remember their behavior at the age of your inner child. They could provide valuable information. They will show you what makes them sad, happy, scared, angry, or ashamed. Pay close attention to your body and what you feel as you watch. Journal your experiences in the following space.

_____

_____

_____

_____

_____

_____

_____

_____

_____

Draw a Picture of Your Inner Child

"Every child is an artist. The problem is how to remain an artist once we grow up."
—**Pablo Picasso**

You do not need to be an artist to draw this picture. You have met your inner wounded child during the meditation. Close your eyes, and remember your meditation and the inner wounded child whom you met. Make your inner child real to you

PARENTING TIPS

The Moon and Your Inner Mother

How often have we heard new parents say, "I wish I had a road map to help guide my child! There are so many books with so many different opinions of how to raise a child. How do I know who and what to believe?" My answer to them is, "You do have that guide: It is their astrological chart." I tell them my experiences about how my astrological chart gave me the answers I needed. I am a good parent to my little girl, because her mother and father needs are delineated and explained in her astrological chart. Understanding the difference between the Moon and Saturn is vital in being a good mother and father. One of the first things you will notice is that your inner child usually requires different energy from each parent. It is a bit daunting to take on such different roles. Our inner mother and father can help when we get stuck. The following parental strategies can support your journey.

Not only does the Moon tell us about the personality of our inner child, but she also provides vital information about our inner mother. You have researched your good and bad mother. Finding our inner good mother connects us to our emotions. She teaches us about the feminine side of us through love and compassion. She wipes away our tears and hugs us when we are scared. She nurtures us. The Moon tells us what kind of mother our inner child needs. I suggest that you become masters of the sign your Moon is in, so that you can become the best mother that you can be to your little child.

Please record your Moon sign again: _____. Locate it in one of the descriptions below, and add your personal responses.

Moon in Aries

- Create a variety of games and creative outlets.
- Encourage them to finish an activity before going to something else.
- Praise them when they are generous and interested in other people.
- Teach them that anger is a normal emotion.
- Help them find personal outlets through which to release their anger. Hitting a punching bag and hitting a pillow with a plastic bat are wonderful ways to express anger.
- Supervise their temper tantrums.
- Discourage their aggression.
- Provide physical activities for you and your inner child that promote competitiveness.

Your Response

Moon in Taurus

- Be patient with them, and explain the value of being patient.
- Maintain consistent boundaries with them.
- Shield them from adult situations that can frighten them.
- Hug and touch them often.
- Praise them for just "being" not doing.
- Remind them of how special they are.
- Provide opportunities for them to cultivate their natural affinity to the Earth. Create a garden with them that is their sanctuary.
- Discourage their bias toward stubbornness.

Your Response

Moon in Gemini

- Talk to your inner child throughout the day.
- Answer all of their questions.
- Read to them before they go to sleep.
- Help them stay focused when they are talking to you.
- Provide them the words to express their feelings.
- Assist them in talking about how they feel.
- Encourage optimism and a belief in serendipity.
- Teach them to live in the present.
- Discourage their bias toward duplicity.

Your Response

Moon in Cancer

- Provide your inner child a warm, loving sanctuary with a sensitive nanny.
- Encourage discussion of feelings.
- Share your feelings with your child.
- Understand and honor their sensitivity and mood swings.
- Help them understand that past hurts do not need to color their present.
- Teach them the power of water as a form of relaxation. Go swimming. Take long baths.
- Give them a toy that will help them feel secure.
- Encourage them to ask for hugs instead of extra food.
- Discourage their closing down emotionally.

Your Response

Moon in Leo

- Create opportunities for your inner child's affinity for drama.
- Discuss the importance of their heart center and how it needs to be nurtured.
- Help them understand the challenges and vulnerability of their need for approval.
- Teach them the importance of connecting with you heart to heart.
- Play, play, play.
- Laugh at their jokes.
- Help your inner child reframe fear into courage.
- Encourage their generous spirit.
- Discourage their bias towards being self-centered.

Your Response

Moon in Virgo

- Encourage your inner child to honor their emotions.
- Help them create an orderly environment.
- Teach them that they are internally perfect and that external excellence is good enough.
- Discuss their challenges with procrastination as a belief in "I have to do it right."
- Celebrate their desire to serve others.
- Remind them that it is not their job to fix other people.
- Provide opportunities for them to understand the challenges of their belief in extremism.
- Reinforce their natural ability to analyze and discriminate life situations.
- Discourage their critical and judgmental attitudes.

Your Response

Moon in Libra

- Encourage them to label and process anger.
- Help them handle their anger privately.
- Encourage their sense of fairness and justice.
- Create a beautiful environment for them.
- Teach them to become more decisive.
- Provide opportunities for them to become independent and assertive.
- Honor their desire to be refined and harmonious.
- Encourage them to honor and respect themselves.
- Teach them that the opinions of others cannot mitigate their belief in themselves.
- Discourage their ambivalence.

Your Response

Moon in Scorpio

- Encourage your inner child to share their intense emotions.
- Honor their secrets.
- Teach them that extremes do not work.
- Provide opportunities that build trust in you.
- Help them when they want to investigate the depths of their emotional life.
- Remind them that life is positive.
- Teach them to be direct in their communication.
- Encourage your inner child to know what they want and need.
- Discourage their bias toward being manipulating.

Your Response

Moon in Sagittarius

- Encourage your inner child's natural optimism and buoyancy.
- Honor their need for freedom.
- Provide opportunities for them to enjoy and explore nature and animals.
- Teach them that their truth is not the only truth.
- Reinforce their desire to understand the meaning of life.
- Create fun things that they can anticipate.
- Honor the philosopher in them.
- Help them look for details when they want to only see the big picture.
- Discourage their bluntness.

Your Response

Moon in Capricorn

- Encourage their emotional expression.
- Teach them ways to become more optimistic
- Create playful activities to bring out the young, happy child
- Respect them and tell them that you do.
- Work with them on creating goals for success.
- Reinforce times when they are open and flexible.
- Honor their desire to be responsible.
- Help them learn ways to relax and remove their mask.
- Discourage their desire to be in control.
- Honor your inner child's innate maturity.

Your Response

Moon in Aquarius

- Encourage your inner child to connect and express their emotions.
- Honor their individuality.
- Help them understand their global connection.
- Understand the times when they are listening to their own internal drummer.
- Acknowledge their unique approach to life situations.
- Respect their social awareness.
- Honor their desire to be independent.
- Teach them to explore unusual ways to resolve their challenges.
- Discourage them from being too detached and aloof.

Your Response

Moon in Pisces

- Honor your inner child's sensitivity.
- Help them understand their vulnerability to other people's feelings.
- Encourage their desire for spirituality.
- Allow them to explore the arts, especially music and dance.
- Provide a spiritual sanctuary for them.
- Help them find ways to control their feelings.
- Teach them how to handle unpleasantness.
- Encourage them to feel good about themselves.
- Discourage their desire to escape from the harsh realities of life.

Your Response

Saturn and Your Inner Father

Saturn is our internal good father. He provides us strong practical foundations through which we become successful. He helps us see the wisdom of finding our own guidance in communicating with our divine source. He brings us back to our basic earthly foundations. He reminds us to honor the earth. He teaches us about personal responsibility and the importance of good boundaries. The planet Saturn tells us what kind of father our inner children need. Paradoxically, it sometimes tells us what we need to be within ourselves and what our external father failed to provide. I rely on the Saturn sign in an astrological chart to give me valuable information concerning the inner child's need for security and safety. Saturn represents the discipline, effort, and reliability that becomes our foundations of character and integrity. It defines structure. It demonstrates how we need to be successful in the real world through understanding the practical realities of life. I would suggest that you become masters of the sign your Saturn is in, so that you can become the best father that you can be to your little child. Please locate your Saturn sign by its glyph and its sign.

Please record your Saturn sign: _____. Locate it in one of the descriptions below, and add your personal responses.

Saturn in Aries

- Teach that true security is within oneself.
- Encourage physical strength.
- Promote a desire for success.
- Reinforce acts of personal responsibility.
- Demonstrate the power of will.
- Allow activities for competitiveness.
- Celebrate moments of self-awareness.
- Encourage independence.
- Create new adventures and new beginnings.
- Teach physical health and discipline.

Your Response

Saturn in Taurus

- Teach the value of the Earth.
- Encourage responsibility to the Earth.
- Create opportunities to improve self-esteem.
- Teach the value of money.
- Acknowledge moments of resourcefulness.
- Celebrate practical creativity.
- Teach boundary setting.
- Encourage integration of spiritual and material values.
- Teach patience and persistence.
- Reinforce finishing projects.
- Teach inner security.
- Provide a safe environment.

Your Response

Saturn in Gemini

- Teach priorities in gathering information.
- Encourage active listening.
- Provide opportunities for focused attention.
- Encourage curiosity.
- Teach personal responsibility for sharing ideas.
- Provide opportunities to label and express emotions.
- Encourage diversity.
- Teach the importance of living in the present.
- Teach clarity in communication.

Your Response

Saturn in Cancer

- Teach the importance of understanding and expressing emotions.
- Encourage the strength to be vulnerable.
- Reinforce sensitivity to others' emotions.
- Provide opportunities for compassion toward others.
- Teach the importance of feminine qualities.
- Encourage self-nurturing.
- Reinforce the relationship with the inner mother.
- Create an emotionally secure environment.

Your Response

Saturn in Leo

- Teach leadership skills.
- Encourage self-respect.
- Provide opportunities for heart connections.
- Teach heart center attributes.
- Honor courage.
- Celebrate humor.
- Encourage innate dramatic ability.
- Provide opportunities to shine.
- Create opportunities to develop self-confidence.
- Reinforce playful activities.

Your Response

Saturn in Virgo

- Encourage internal perfection.
- Teach the importance of service to others.
- Teach organizational skills.
- Encourage health habits.
- Celebrate analytic skills.
- Create opportunities for discrimination.
- Teach the power of third options.
- Encourage the understanding of emotions.

Your Response

Saturn in Libra

- Teach the need for balance.
- Encourage mediation and negotiation.
- Reinforce innate sense of fairness.
- Celebrate desire for beauty.
- Create a peaceful environment.
- Encourage responsibility for self.
- Teach decision-making techniques.
- Encourage relationship with self.
- Encourage natural relationship interests.

Your Response

Saturn in Scorpio

- Teach responsibility for wants and desires.
- Encourage passion.
- Celebrate the pursuit of success.
- Encourage mastery of emotions.
- Celebrate probing mysteries.
- Teach belief in transformation.
- Help understand others' values.
- Encourage an attitude of positive outcomes.

Your Response

Saturn in Sagittarius

- Support natural philosophic affinity.
- Provide opportunities to discover personal truth.
- Encourage travel needs.
- Reinforce honesty.
- Teach the big picture.
- Encourage responsibility to teaching and sharing ideas.
- Encourage the search for meaning.
- Answer religious questions.

Your Response

Saturn in Capricorn

- Teach responsibility for success.
- Encourage respect for authority.
- Celebrate moments of maturity.
- Encourage ambition.
- Teach congruence.
- Encourage order and efficiency.
- Celebrate moments of wisdom.
- Teach goal setting.
- Encourage loyalty.
- Teach the wisdom of understanding emotions.

Your Response

Saturn in Aquarius

- Encourage equality.
- Encourage cause orientation.
- Celebrate visionary goals.
- Honor uniqueness.
- Encourage individuality.
- Teach the importance of friendship.
- Celebrate affinity to humanism.

Your Response

Saturn in Pisces

- Teach the mastery of emotions.
- Encourage a sense of self-value.
- Encourage spiritual nature.
- Celebrate creative talents.
- Honor psychic gifts.
- Teach spiritual awareness.
- Teach the importance of the unconscious (dreams).
- Provide opportunities for compassionate service.

Your Response

Meditation: Inner Divine Mother and Father

Michael Brady's guided hypnotic meditation will enable you to experience a visceral, emotional relationship with your inner divine mother and father. Allow yourself a half hour to be quiet and still with no external interruptions. Listen to the second meditation and meet your inner divine mother and father. Journal your experiences in the space provided below. This meditation can be found at KarmicFreedom.com/Store available for purchase to accompany this chapter.

Inner Divine Mother Notes

Inner Divine Father Notes

Inner Parents Worksheet

My inner child was hurt because my mother was:

Example: I have a Moon in Pisces. My mother worked my entire childhood. She was often very tired when she came home. I was raised by my Aunt Marion. My inner child felt abandoned by her mother. She wanted to be nurtured by her. She learned to be a good little girl who sacrificed her needs to be praised. Her mother taught her that it was better to give than to receive, so she became a little healer and martyr.

_____

_____

_____

_____

_____

_____

_____

_____

_____

_____

_____

_____

_____

I can be a responsible inner mother to my inner child by:

Example: I have a Moon in Pisces. I can acknowledge her sensitivity and empathy. I can teach her how to use her emotional skills to serve herself as well as others. I can foster her creativity. I can honor her spiritual nature and provide time when she can be still and quiet. I can talk and listen to her. I will never abandon her. I will tell her that she is a good girl just because she lives. I will help her love herself.

Your Commitment Letter

I have cautioned many of my clients not to make a half-hearted commitment to developing a relationship with their inner child. They have been ignored and abandoned for years. Bringing them out of the closet they have lived in and giving them hope for a relationship is wonderful. Changing your mind and breaking your commitment would break their heart. You now know your inner mother and father. You have read parenting tips for your inner child. If you are serious, the commitment will last the rest of your life. When you are ready, I recommend writing a letter to your inner child, telling them how much you love them and want to be their good parent.

My Dear Child,

_____

_____

_____

_____

_____

_____

_____

_____

_____

_____

_____

_____

_____

_____

With much love,

Your Name

THE SANCTUARY

Creating the Sanctuary

My little girl needs to be protected. As a child, even at 3, she was given the role of mediator. She was handling situations too adult for a little girl. When the police found the mentally challenged teenager who had abused her, she said, "Please don't hurt him, he is not as smart as me." She volunteered at a hospital for special needs children when she was 9 years old. She was taught early on to give rather than to receive. She was thrown into the frontlines of life, which is abusive for a small Pisces child. She did not know that she needed to be protected from the slings and arrows of the world. When I became aware of her, she still did not know. She was a smart, adultlike, controlling child who thought she could take care of everyone.

It took me months of talking, cajoling, and boundary setting for her to learn that there were life situations that were inappropriate and impossible for a 3-year-old to fix. Together we created a sanctuary, a magical day care center for her when I was busy with adult business. It has mostly worked. She sneaks out often. She believes that she should be able to help me with my clients. She actually believes that she is a better counselor than I am. I have to be conscious of her wiles and send her back to her sanctuary.

Her sanctuary is quite wonderful. Her nanny is her beloved Aunt Marion. All of her dogs are there. She can play in the woods all day long. She has friends, but she prefers to be with Lassie, her collie, or with Pal, her little mutt. She has a cottage ringed by evergreens, where she often sits and thinks about magical things. She is a good singer, so she practices there. She especially loves "The Lord's Prayer." It is her signature song when she performs. She loves her sanctuary, but she gets bored very easily. She is, however, much happier and certainly more at peace there.

She was a pleasantly plump little girl who ate sweets

all day long. She still wants to do that. I could not allow her to do that. This has been a war that has been active for many years.

During the time Michael and I lived in Vermont, we would often visit the hardware store, which had the best soft ice cream I have ever tasted. Lynnie thought so too and wanted one when we went into town. When I began my diet to lose 130 pounds, I could not afford to eat soft ice cream. Lynnie was mad. Each time we drove by the hardware store, she had a fit. It was becoming a real issue for me. One day, I decided to give her what she wanted. I told her that I was going to give her a dollar to buy her own ice cream cone. We would watch her as she walked to the store and got the largest ice cream you can imagine. She was delighted, and off we went to the hardware store. Michael and I sat in the car and watched her buy her ice cream. The key to this experience was that Lynnie was doing all of this in my mind. She took her prize and went into her sanctuary. She got what she wanted, and I do not have to deal with the calories.

My inner parents have made very good use of the sanctuary, and I know you can too. Many of my clients find it hard to imagine that this inner child who resides so deep in us can be put in a place outside of us. I believe in the power of my mind to create everything Lynnie and I need. Trust in the process, and you and your inner child can create a wonderful sanctuary. I know that the power of the sanctuary was critical in the weight loss that probably saved my life.

Sanctuary Meditation

Michael Brady's guided hypnotic meditation will enable you to create a beautiful sanctuary for your inner child. Allow yourself a half hour to be quiet and still with no external interruptions. Listen to the third meditation and begin to create your child's sanctuary. This meditation can be found at KarmicFreedom.com/Store available for purchase to accompany this chapter.

Sanctuary Meditation Notes

YOUR INNER JOYFUL CHILD

"The real you is still a little child who never grew up. Sometimes that little child comes out when you are having fun or playing, when you feel happy, when you are painting, or writing poetry, or playing the piano, or expressing yourself in some way. These are the happiest moments of your life - when the real you comes out, when you don't care about the past and you don't worry about the future. You are childlike."

—Miguel Angel Ruiz

I did a radio show a while ago. The host asked me why it was so important for me to create a relationship with my inner child. The first thing that popped in my mind was a moment on Jay Peak Mountain in Jay, Vermont. My little girl was pretending to be a goat climbing a mountain. She was giggling about that as she climbed quickly over a rock. I had forgotten how physically creative I used to be at that age. I spent all of my young life walking the woods, building dams on the stream, and making forts. I would imagine myself a horse, a dog, a lion. I wanted to be in nature, my sacred space! I was thrilled at being able to feel that creative again. Pure fun and physical enjoyment.

Most of the clients in my practice are willing to take on the responsibility of parenting their inner child, yet there are those who say, "I don't care. I've raised my kids and I'm done parenting." Then they say, "I just want to be happy now." That is my opening to suggesting how inner child work may help them be happy. My response is: "Who do you think in you is the part of you that's happy?" They look at me, questioning, "What's a part?" I respond, "The inner child is the part of you that's happy or sad. And it's not a 'just '"To be happy, you need to get in touch with your inner child. We all want to be happy, but how can we be happy if our inner children are wounded and miserable? To feel joy, we have to have our emotional channels open: open to sadness, open to anger, open to all feelings. Some people are afraid to look at their pain and their suffering, and they choose not to look at it. Those people are emotionally blocked. As you do your inner child work and discover and embrace your emotions, you also experience joy.

I had been walking every day to help me lose weight for a year. I was able to walk four or five miles a day up and down the Jay Peak Mountains. Somewhere in that time, I was welcoming Lynnie to walk with me. She was enjoying the physical feelings and the competition with herself and with Michael. One day, we were doing our usual walk and decided to change it up a bit. That meant walking up a very steep hill that was about 1/4 miles up. This particular day, she wanted to be in charge of walking up that hill. She wanted to beat Michael up the hill. She had never done that. That day, she made it up minutes before Michael. She stood at the top of the hill, laughing and shouting, "I am an athlete too, Mommy!"

The adult me was so proud of her and glad there was no one else around. Imagine a woman standing at the top of a hill, screaming at her mommy that she was an athlete. That day was a turning point for us. The next day, we were at the country store where Miss Peggy made and sold homemade cupcakes. Lynnie wanted one and started her rant. This time, I took her outside and said, "Sweetie, athletes don't eat cupcakes, and you are an athlete, aren't you?" She smiled and shook her little head, "Yes, Mommy, I am an athlete, too." It has been our standing joke ever since.

Your Favorite Childhood Activities

"Within us all is a radiant inner child bathed in joy."

—Amy Leigh Mercree

Your preferences can reflect your inner child's thoughts, desires, and emotions. Read those old books. Rent and watch those old movies and television shows. Remember how they made you feel.

Favorite Books

1. _____
2. _____
3. _____
4. _____
5. _____
6. _____

Movies

1._____

2._____

3._____

4._____

5._____

6._____

Television

1._____

2._____

3._____

4._____

5._____

6._____

Indoor Games

1._____

2._____

3._____

4._____

5._____

6._____

Outdoor Games

1._____

2._____

3._____

4._____

5._____

6._____

Your Best Friends

1._____

2._____

3._____

4._____

5._____

6._____

Meditation: Your Inner Joyful Child

Michael Brady's guided hypnotic meditation will enable you to experience a visceral, emotional relationship with your unconscious mind. Your inner joyful child lives there. Allow yourself a half hour to be quiet and still with no external interruptions. Listen to the fourth meditation and meet your inner joyful child. Journal your experiences in the space provided below. This meditation can be found at KarmicFreedom.com/Store available for purchase to accompany this chapter.

_____

_____

_____

_____

_____

_____

_____

_____

Draw a Picture of the Joyful Child

You do not need to be an artist to draw this picture. Have fun with it! Remember how creative you used to be. You have met your inner joyful child during the meditation. Close your eyes, and remember your meditation and the inner child that you met. Allow your inner child to help you draw a picture of him or her. Make your inner child real to you

YOUR INNER CHILD AND DREAMING

The Value of Dreaming

> *"The dream is the small hidden door in the deepest and most intimate sanctum of the soul, which opens into that primeval cosmic night that was soul long before there was conscious ego and will be soul far beyond what a conscious ego could ever reach."*
>
> —**Carl Jung**

Through the unconscious mind, the soul provides us with answers to all of life's questions by deluging us with hundreds of symbols. Jung defines the unconscious, in The Structure and Dynamics of the Psyche, as: "Everything of which I know, but of which I am not at the moment thinking; everything of which I was once conscious, but have now forgotten; everything perceived by my senses, but not noted by my conscious mind; everything which, involuntarily and without paying attention to it, I feel, think, remember, want and do; all the future things that are taking shape in me and will sometime come to consciousness; all this is the content of the unconscious."

To Jung's definition I would add that the unconscious contains memories not only from this life but from other lives as well. Our unconscious minds project all of the wisdom gleaned from previous incarnations through the language of symbology. The unconscious part of our personality also contains many of the undesirable traits we consciously reject and, therefore, repress. Jung referred to this as the Shadow. Afraid of the dark, unseemly memories that we might unearth and the havoc that they might wreak, many of us fear our unconscious mind. However, it is the converse that is true: What we don't know can hurt us. Your unconscious mind can be your best friend, a warehouse of information that you want to bring to consciousness.

The challenge is how to access that information. The source of the difficulty is that our unconscious mind has no direct communication with our conscious mind, which means that we can explore its knowledge only indirectly. Moreover, while our conscious mind provides us with information more literally, the language of our unconscious mind is largely symbolic. To pursue our unconscious mind's vast information, we must use processes that include astrology, dream interpretation, and various forms of symbology. Analyzing our dreams can be an illuminating and insightful experience, as long as we know how to interpret the symbols provided. Numerous theories and books on the subject of dream analysis abound, but my view is simple: Like Jung, I believe that everything in your dream is a reflection of you. I also believe that there is a correlation between your dream symbology and your astrological symbols.

Using both provides an enormous amount of relevant data. Before I show you how it works, let's consider a few symbolic structures.

What role does sex play in a dream? Usually,

whichever sex you dream about is the part of you that you need to explore. If you're female and have a dream about a man, then he is a manifestation of your male side. If you're male dreaming about a woman, the converse is true. If the man in your dream is angry, it could mean that you need to look at the anger that you've been hiding from yourself. This approach can be somewhat unsettling, because our dreams can portray the players as nightmarish. You may find it difficult to believe that the garish person in your dream could represent any part of yourself. If, however, you are experiencing the same types of conflicts in your waking life, you need to be able to claim those behaviors and take responsibility for them. Suppose, for example, that you're a man and have been having periodic dreams about your Aunt Bianca. Aunt Bianca is now a representation of your female side. You want to discover more about that hidden side, so you analyze Aunt Bianca's behaviors in your dreams.

In your list of her characteristics, you notice that one

in particular causes you some discomfort: her tendency to be somewhat clingy and dependent. Perhaps the hidden female in you has a tendency to be clingy and dependent. Maybe, in your waking life, you attract women who are clingy and dependent, a tendency that you find deplorable but unalterable. Dreaming about Aunt Bianca has given you a phenomenal gift: You are now aware of the female part of you that you can explore and change to help create a resolution.

Houses are a common dream symbol. They are separated into floors: The basement can represent what is not known to us—our unconscious; the first floor can be our ego or personality; and the attic, our spiritual side. Houses also can be seen as an opportunity to put the dream in the context of time: Old houses often symbolize past life memories, as do houses that we perceive as ours in our dream but in actuality aren't. Various parts of a house and its surroundings are also significant and correspond to specific astrological characteristics.

The following list will give you an idea of the correspondence between the parts of a house and the astrological signs:

- Aries: doorway, any entrance like an anteroom, reception rooms
- Taurus: garden, furniture
- Gemini: hallway, telephone, garage
- Cancer: kitchen, family room, water faucet
- Leo: children's room, game room, television room
- Virgo: bathroom, shower, laundry
- Libra: art and decorations, living room
- Scorpio: septic system, toilet
- Sagittarius: balcony, deck, library, attic
- Capricorn: formal dining room, roof, home office
- Aquarius: electrical wiring and appliances, computers
- Pisces: drainage system

If You Have Trouble Remembering Your Dreams

Many of my clients have difficulty remembering their dreams. Here are a few tips that can help. First and foremost, make a commitment to recalling your dreams by keeping a dream journal. Have it available by your bed. As soon as you wake up, jot down any remembrance, no matter how small. If you dislike writing in a journal, have a tape recorder there, and record yourself describing the dream. Give yourself time in the morning to remember. Before you go to sleep each night, ask your soul to aid you in remembering your dreams. Let it know that you are ready to know what memories are stored in your unconscious mind—that you are not afraid. Another helpful hint is to spend a few minutes thinking about your day before you sleep. This way your dreams will be more than just a mundane review of your day.

People who have difficulty remembering their dreams are usually reluctant to deal with their unconscious mind on other levels. They may be afraid of the information stored there, preferring the "what-I-don't-know-won't-hurt-me" approach. By having the courage to listen to their unconscious, however, they would live happier, more fulfilling lives. Thomas Edison, just one of a score of notable personalities who believed that answers could be mined from our unconscious, would "sleep" on a problem involving one of his inventions.

Your inner child resides in your unconscious mind and in your emotional body. One of the most effective methods to connect with him or her is through your dreams. It occurred to me that I need to give you my perspective on dreams and their value before asking you to use them to access your inner child. I believe that dreams are a gift from our soul and God. A dream can be an answer to a spoken or unspoken prayer. Through dreams, we are able to listen to the voice of God. Dreams help us to access the riches of our unconscious minds. Mining these depths provides us with the symbols necessary to understand our past and current lives in highly creative ways.

You know your inner child's astrological personality from reading about your Moon sign. The symbols that derive from that information provide important insights into understanding your child. For example, a Moon in Sagittarius child might dream of a young horse running free in a pasture; a Moon in Pisces child could dream of a small goldfish being pursued by larger fish; a Moon in Leo child might dream of lion cubs abandoned by their mother. Other more obvious symbols are dreaming of children in various situations interacting with different people.

The key to the dream process is to ask your soul for information about your little one on an ongoing basis. Now that you are more familiar with the personality of your inner child, you are more ready to take on the role of good mother and good father. Because your inner child is very unconscious, another way to help get in touch with them is through your dreams. There is a chapter in our book Discovering Your Soul Mission: New Rules for a New Age that explores dream symbology. In addition, each night, ask your soul for dream symbols that will provide you the information that you need. The following questions will assist you in programming your dreams to learn more about your inner child.

How would you describe your inner child?

What can you do to parent your inner child?

How can you best nurture your adult self?

How do you express your emotions?

What do you need to feel safe?

How do you separate yourself from others?

What emotional beliefs do you need to change?

What early habits do you need to change?

How would you describe your relationship with your mother?

How important is your physical home?

Two Dream Examples and Interpretations

Steve's Dream

"I dreamt of a small male child about 5 years old who was struggling under water in a large lake. A woman pulls him out of the water and places him on a sidewalk with many houses on both sides of the street. The child is confused but soon chooses a small blue house on the left side of the street, walks up to the door, and knocks, but no one answers. He is crying and no one hears him."

Steve is one of my male clients who has a Moon in Cancer. Cancer rules water, especially lakes. In the dream, the small male child symbolizes his inner child, who is struggling with bringing his emotions to the surface. Steve's mother died when he was 5 years old. He is confused by this loss and afraid of the depths of his emotional pain. He is trying to find his way to a place where he feels nurtured enough to ameliorate that pain. The house is on the left side of the street, which symbolizes the past. The color is blue, a Cancer color that represents the deep feelings and sensitivities of that sign. He finds a house but no one answers him. He is sad with no one to comfort him. Clearly, this is Steve's inner child trying to get his attention. He needs his mother and has for years. The woman in the dream is Steve's inner divine Mother, whom he needs to help his inner child feel safe and happy. He has within himself the ability to be a nurturing, loving, and compassionate mother to his 5-year-old inner child.

Peter's Dream

"I walk into a room and witness a man abusing and molesting a small child. The man turns and looks at me and says, with absolute contempt and arrogance: 'Oh, you are in the wrong place at the wrong time.' For a moment, I feel this absolute fear. Then, as I glance at the child, in a split second, it changes to anger and rage. I step forward and grab the man and snap his neck with my bare hands. He's dead. I scoop up the child in my arms and get us out of there. End of dream."

The interpretation of this troubling dream seems apparent and important. Peter was, in fact, that man abusing that small child. He had wanted his inner child to die and the man was trying to kill the child. He saved the child and transformed the bad man. He learned how to protect the child.

Now his story, in his words:

I've come from a place of being more intellectual than emotional. This place, at times, even made me wish my inner child would just die so that I wouldn't have to deal with his emotions. Through my work with Linda and Michael, I have come to understand that my initial reaction, to ignore and not care for my inner child, hurt me emotionally. It also kept me from really enjoying life. I've come to understand that I must first nurture my inner child to actually love myself and create the life my heart desires.

Techniques for Better Dreaming

(Use my sample dream journal in the Addendum. Plan to sleep more.)

- ❖ Keep a dream journal. Have it handy. (See Addendum for sample journal.) Record everything that you remember, even if it is only a snippet of information. Do not make judgments about what is important or interesting. Everything that our unconscious minds give us is sacred and important.
- ❖ Program yourself to awaken at 90-minute intervals during the night (for a short period of time to activate your memories). Record what you remember. Our REM periods occur at approximately 90-minute intervals from the time that we fall asleep.
- ❖ Perform a pre-sleep ritual. Read your dream journal from nights before to focus you on your dream goals. Set the alarm for 15 minutes earlier than your regular wake-up time. Review your day so that your dreams

are not fragments of the day's events. Ask your soul to bring you the dreams that you need and want.

- ❖ Perform a ritual each morning. Your first thought in the morning should be: "What was I dreaming?" Do not get up or move. Do not think about your day's schedule. Cling to any thoughts or clues about what you were dreaming. Pull out the feelings and images. Describe them in your journal. If you cannot recall anything, record your feelings upon awakening.

Meditation for Better Sleep and Dreaming

Michael Brady's guided hypnotic meditation will enable you to experience a visceral, connection to your unconscious mind. You will experience better sleep and have more lucid dreams. Allow yourself a half hour to be quiet and still with no external interruptions. Listen to the fifth meditation. Journal your experiences in the space provided below. This meditation can be found at KarmicFreedom.com/Store available for purchase to accompany this chapter.

YOUR INNER CHILD AND YOUR ADULT RELATIONSHIPS

Couples often come to work with Michael and me for holistic coaching before and during their marriages. We tell them from the beginning of our work together that we will be working with at least four people: Their two adults and two inner children will become obvious in our journey. They are, of course, surprised and a bit skeptical. Soon, they realize the power of their unconscious children in causing disruptions in their relationship. Children, by nature, do not want to be in a relationship like a marriage, for one thing. They just want to be with their parents. Young inner children are very self-centered. They start learning about playmates when they're 5, 6, or 7 years old, when they start to understand that they can exist separately from their families and go out and develop other relationships.

That doesn't happen at age 3. Children at that age are not one bit interested in our marriages, and they're often jealous because of the attention that we're giving to a partner, especially if they think that we are not giving them any. This kind of behavior often has a negative effect on relationships. Our old feelings tend to come up and play out in our relationships. I have some very intellectual clients who are as unsophisticated in marriage as any two people can be. They get into fights, and they are like kids in a sandbox, yelling and screaming at each other. I'll tell them they're acting like children, and they'll agree. Both sides do it, not just one or the other. They are emotionally immature when they allow their inner children to be in charge. As stated earlier in this book, we've all had moments in our lives when we said or did something that, afterward, we could not believe we said or did. Some things come out as really immature and childish.

We have our clients learn about their inner children, parent them, and stop projecting their child selves onto each other. We recommend playdates with their inner children to create a childlike connection. These relationships and what they learn from their inner children create wonderful opportunities to be better parents to their biological children. Using their children's astrological charts, they can determine what their children desire in their good mothers and fathers. They learn about their children what their needs and wants really are. Now you have a guidebook for them and for your inner child.

YOUR KARMIC CHILD

I believe that, on an unconscious level, your personality links you to the seminal belief system you learned from your parents; the hidden child within you; memories and pain that have not been dealt with in your conscious life; and your night dreams, fears, and phobias. This deep level also remembers personalities you've had from other lives and important information about who and what you have been. These memories of the thoughts, actions, and feelings of previous personalities share a common thread with you now, and they become the source of much of your unconscious motivation, impulse, angst, and relationship challenges.

Your soul, in its infinite wisdom, has chosen your mother and father to provide you with very significant karmic information. Karma is complete only when we have balanced our previous actions through consciousness, commitment, and new actions. Our soul knows these situations and relationships and will create opportunities for us to resolve them. Our astrological chart, created by our soul, provides us with information about these karmic experiences as a spiritual reminder, a road map to understanding.

Imagine yourself as a soul on the other side. You are preparing to incarnate back to the earth plane. You meet with other souls to plan the relationships that you will need to fulfill your life's purpose. You speak to the soul, for instance, who is to be your father in your next earthly existence. Together, you recall your previous life experiences, as well as the conflicts that will need to be resolved and the obligations that will need to be met. You acknowledge the love that has endured throughout time. You decide on the context of the relationship you will share to help both of you evolve. Your souls co-created a soul contract. You have many meetings like this one to consummate all the contracts you need to evolve and grow spiritually in your next life.

Your soul then integrates your soul contracts into your astrological chart. Information in the chart reminds you of the contracts and the souls with whom you've contracted.

That vague sense of "knowing" or familiarity we experience when we meet new people can be attributed to the fact that we usually don't recognize the personalities behind our soul agreements, but we always recognize their souls. Our soul knows the people we're going to bring into our lives. Our astrological chart only serves as a blueprint of what our soul intends for us to help us evolve. We might not recognize someone immediately, but if we have some notion of what our soul needs us to learn in this life, the reasons for their presence in our life will become more readily apparent.

I remember teaching a workshop years ago on karmic contracts. I suggested that our souls create relationships with our parents to learn great karmic lessons. A man in the audience raised his hand and, after being called on, said, "Well, I must have been drunk when I 'created' my father!"

Everyone laughed. The truth is that his father was perfect; it just did not feel that way. He needed his problematic father to remind him of previous lives when he had been abusive. His astrological chart said that he would need to go through that to be free of the past by creating karmic balance and opportunities for resolution. My stepfather would often say to me in drunken anger that I was a liar and the truth was not in me. He told this to a little girl who had never lied in her young life. She loved telling the truth, even if it got her into trouble. Years later, after becoming an astrologer, I discovered I had Saturn in Gemini. The interpretation was that, in a previous life, I had used words to manipulate people and steal their written work and had lied to get out of trouble. I was, in fact, an abusive cosmic used car salesman.

Saturn shows us what we have been as people in other lives. It also described men who would become our fathers. My stepfather was telling me who I had been and why I had attracted him into my life this time. "You are a liar, and the truth is not in you" would provide me with significant clues about who I was as a man in past lives. It also proved to me that I had, in fact, chosen him and created an astrological placement that would help me resolve my past.

The problem is that our little ones are hearing all of these hateful statements and are unable to understand why they are being so hurt. I remember so many dinners when Doug screamed those words to me. It would make me cry. Once, I stood up against him and told him he was wrong, but that led to more verbal abuse and would cause me to be silent. Children become the containers for all forms of reactive emotional abuse. They carry those judgments, criticism, and anger with them as unconscious beliefs. These beliefs transform into lack of self-esteem and self-value, which can ruin their lives. They feel shame and guilt that they are unable to explain.

Our job is to discover the essence of their karmic experiences and help them resolve those issues to be free. I believe that we all suffer from karmic posttraumatic stress syndrome. We have all had traumatic past lives and carry so many unresolved feelings in our unconscious minds around our past experiences. We need to deal with what we're holding onto and why we're holding onto those feelings so that we can release them.

CONCLUSION: BECOMING THE SPIRITUAL ADULT

Over dinner with my friend, Anne, I told her about an important event that occurred with me several years ago. She asked if I have included it in this book. I had not and was surprised I had forgotten it. 'Please write it, Linda it could be life-changing for your readers." .I will leave you with that story. I needed to have a face lift after losing 130 pounds. I had a triple chin and no definition in my face. In my initial consult with my surgeon, he mentioned a bump on my forehead. I told him I have had it my whole life. I believed everyone had a bump. I was amazed when I asked Michael where his bump was and he said he did not have one. I began to notice that no one had one. My doctor told me that it might have been the result of a fall that could have cracked my skull. Then I remembered falling down the stairs several times when I was very young. I do not remember the pain. Two days after my surgery I was able to look at my face. My bump was gone! I was amazed and later questioned my doctor. I will never forget the look on his face when he said 'Linda I took it away when I did your face-lift. You do not need it anymore!" He had removed years of painful memories with his act of generosity. I will say to you "Your inner child does not need them anymore!"

In the last chapter of our book Discovering Your Soul Mission: New Rules for a New Age, we wrote the following: There will be a time when we are the "man" and the "woman" to our inner family and good parents to our younger selves. There will be a time when we honor and respect ourselves as much as we do others. There will be a time when we claim our gift from God – our soul – to strengthen and empower us to greatness. There will be a time when we and our souls are the foundations of our spiritual lives and that our religious community is sourced by that knowledge. There will be a time when security is measured by our will to succeed and to pursue our spiritual missions. I believe that spiritual adulthood is also predicated on understanding the incredible diversity of our inner lives. To me one of most important parts we need to investigate, welcome and nurture is the child who lives within.

You have spent time reading, analyzing your astrological chart, meditating, and dreaming about your precious inner child. You may have finished your 1-month challenge. Now, it is time to go back and do your earlier assessment and see how far you have come. Congratulations! You are on the journey to becoming a spiritually, mature adult. Your deep connection to your inner divine family is making you whole and happy. Please remember your commitment to your little one, and spend your life in a relationship that will bring you joy.

ADDENDUM

Astrological Symbolism

♈ Aries

Symbol: The Ram
Element: Fire
Key Phrase: I Am

♈ Energies

- Self-aware
- Creative
- Pioneer
- Takes action
- Confident
- Energetic
- Risk-taker
- Assertive
- Deals with anger
- Physical
- Loves new beginnings
- Courage
- Alert
- Stimulating
- Explorer

- Selfish
- Impulsive
- Accident prone
- Impatient
- Combative
- Reckless
- Abusive
- Quick-tempered
- Easily bored
- No follow-through
- Arrogant
- Domineering
- Self-willed
- Fearful

♈ Common Symbols

Red, fire, East, Spring, #1, knifes and other sharp objects, the desert, ram, firemen, soldiers, daybreak, battles, Moses, matches, lighters, karate and other martial arts, surgery and surgeons

♉ Taurus

Symbol:	The Bull
Element:	Earth
Key Phrase:	I Have

♉ Energies

- Sensual
- Tactile
- Builders
- Practically creative
- Stable
- Patient
- Finisher
- Earthy
- Loyal
- Artistic
- Warm
- Values self
- Dependable
- Placid
- Serene
- Needs security
- Fearful of change
- Stuck
- Stubborn
- Materialistic
- Obstinate
- Slow moving
- Self-indulgent
- Indolent
- Lazy
- Possessive
- Stingy
- Over-/under-estimates worth
- Complacent
- Fear of poverty
- Vain

♉ Common Symbols

Green, earth, #2, the bull, the Buddha, potters, bankers, money, plants, landscapers, gardeners, easy chairs, investments, singers, soft materials like silk and velvet, bank deposits, wallets, practical art, cooking, building

♏ Scorpio

Symbol: The Scorpion
Element: Water
Key Phrase: I Desire

♏ Energies

- Sexual
- Powerful
- Intense
- Insightful
- Investigator
- Mysterious
- Emotional
- Strong willed
- Passionate
- Probing
- Inscrutable
- Controlled
- Transforming
- Knows desires
- Loyal
- Spiritual rebirth

- Likes suffering
- Vindictive
- Revengeful
- Extreme
- Judgmental
- Scheming
- Sarcastic
- Paranoid
- Intimidating
- Withholding
- Secretive
- Distrustful
- Jealous
- Controlling
- Repressed
- Obsessive

♏ Common Symbols

Black, white, or dark red, water, #8, hidden and dark places, researchers, tornadoes, funerals, insurance, sexuality, psychiatrists, nuclear weapons, Niagara Falls, loans, deep water, scorpions, eagles and doves, magic

♊ Gemini

Symbol: The Twins
Element: Air
Key Phrase: I Think

♊ Energies

- Bright
- Gathers information
- Versatile
- Curious
- Alert
- Movement oriented
- Cognitive
- Literary
- In the now
- Writer
- Responsiveness
- Adaptable
- Communicative
- Dualistic
- Eloquent

- Restless
- Gossipy
- Moody
- Inconsistent
- Hard to relax
- Overly talkative
- Detached
- Lost in the now
- Scattered
- Unfocused
- Changeable
- Impatient
- Impractical
- Superficiality
- Duplicitous
- Loses big picture

♊ Common Symbols

Yellow, air, #3, twins, wind, cars, newspapers, journalists, books, birds, traffic signs, a watch, libraries, con men, writing material, speech therapists, respiratory therapists

♐ Sagittarius

Symbol: The Archer
Element: Fire
Key Phrase: I Understand

♐ Energies

- Truthful
- Spiritual
- Traveler
- Philosopher
- Inspiring
- Futuristic
- Freedom
- Ethical
- Optimistic
- Naturalist
- Generous
- Enlightened
- Intuitive
- Sense of humor
- Spiritual goals
- Wise
- Idealistic

- Dogmatic
- Impractical
- Overly abstract
- Outspoken
- Unrealistic
- Commitment phobic
- Too expansive
- Irresponsible
- Preachy
- Restless
- Claustrophobic
- Extravagant
- Procrastinating
- Whimsical
- Pollyanna
- Too global

♐ Common Symbols

Purple, fire, #9, horses, gambling, mountains, sports, law, arrows, colleges, luck, the future, clergy, publications, bachelors, lawyers, anything that deals with expansion

♋ Cancer

Symbol:	The Crab
Element:	Water
Key Phrase:	I Feel

♋ Energies

- Emotional
- Sensitive
- Maternal
- Vulnerable
- Childlike
- Empathetic
- Home loving
- Intuitive
- Values the past
- Supportive
- Loyal
- Devoted to family
- Protective
- Traditional
- Patriotic
- Nurturing

- Insecure
- Hypersensitive
- Smothering
- Indulgent
- Pathetic
- Moody/touchy
- Insecure
- Clings to past
- Passive/timid
- Withholding
- Childish
- Obsessed with being needed
- Manipulative
- Fears change
- Dependent
- Shy

♋ Common Symbols

Silver blue, water, #4, crabs, lakes, mothers, containers that hold liquid, milk, boats, food, cooks, historians, sailors, restaurants, and homes

♑ Capricorn

Symbol: The Goat
Element: Earth
Key Phrase: I Use

♑ Energies

- Responsible
- Reserved
- Cautious
- Structured
- Loyal
- Committed
- Executive
- Father-like
- Hardworking
- Realistic
- Traditional
- Self-reliant
- Disciplined
- Ambitious
- Integrity
- Professional
- Prudent

- Arrogant
- Pessimistic
- Overly cautious
- Rigid
- Inflexible
- Calculating
- Authoritarian
- Obsessed with rules
- Remote
- Materialistic
- Severe
- Insensitive
- Difficulty with feeling
- Unforgiving
- Stubborn

♑ Common Symbols

Brown, earth, South, Winter, #10, fathers, authority figures, older, wiser people, grandfather clocks, government, CEOs, calendars, foundations, antiques, big business, boundaries

♌ Leo

Symbol: The Lion
Element: Fire
Key Phrase: I Will

♌ Energies

- Proud/regal
- Generous
- Dramatic
- Fun loving
- Childlike
- Youthful
- Leader
- Self-respect
- Confident
- Inspiring
- Spontaneous
- Commanding
- Powerful
- Magnetism
- Will
- Likeable
- Warm

- Insecure
- Arrogant
- Melodramatic
- Self-indulgent
- Status conscious
- Fear of aging
- Autocratic
- Needs center stage
- Never serious
- Needs constant love

♌ Common Symbols

Gold, fire, #5, actor, theater, crowns, television, games, children, Sun, vacations, parties, movies, kings, thrones, fun, lottery, all glamorous things, holidays, lions

♒ Aquarius

Symbol: The Water-bearer
Element: Air
Key Phrase: I Know

♒ Energies

- Individual
- Futuristic
- Innovative
- Humanist
- Open-minded
- Rational
- Scientific
- Unique
- Independent
- Reformer
- Cooperative
- Philosophic
- Original
- Friendliness
- Need for groups
- Networker
- Cause oriented

- Rebellious
- Non-conformist
- Cold
- Repressed
- Detached
- Impersonal
- Too logical
- Erratic
- Inflexible
- Uninvolved
- Distant
- Intolerant
- Too observing
- Temperamental
- Discontent
- Indifferent
- Aloof

♒ Common Symbols

Electric blue, air, #11, airplanes, computers, astrology, new technology, politics, voluntarism, causes, revolutionary ideas, inventors, teams approach, space, like-minded people

♍ Virgo

Symbol: The Virgin
Element: Earth
Key Phrase: I Analyze

♍ Energies

- Discriminates
- Analytical
- Logical
- Practical
- Service oriented
- Healthy
- Efficient
- Organized
- Thorough
- Dependable
- Conscientious
- Seek perfection
- Precise
- Scientific
- Modest
- Humility

- Hypercritical
- Workaholic
- Self-critical
- Picky/petty
- Martyr-like
- Hypochondriac
- Extreme
- Perfectionistic
- Obsessive
- Worrying
- Doesn't take criticism well
- Judgmental
- Melancholy
- Pessimistic
- Nagging
- Inadequate

♍ Common Symbols

White, earth, #6, health foods, doctors, nurses, nutritionists, lists and programs that create order, organized labor, soap, virgins, wheat, cleaning supplies, small animals, chores, tests, homework

♓ Pisces

Symbol: Two Fish
Element: Water
Key Phrase: I Believe

♓ Energies

- Spiritual
- Artistic
- Sensitive
- Flowing
- Adapting
- Idealistic
- Romantic
- Reflective
- Sacrificing
- Forgiving
- Empathetic
- Compassion
- Serene
- Emotional
- Introspection
- Psychic
- Musical

- Escapist
- Daydreamer
- Martyr-like
- Cowardly
- Overly sensitive
- Illusionary
- Illogical
- Dependent
- Self-pitying
- Too submissive
- Naïve
- Lazy
- Pessimistic
- Addictive
- Self-destructive

♓ Common Symbols

Lavender, water, #12, ocean, whales and dolphins, alcohol, drugs, dreams, psychics, martyrs, ballet, retreats, illusions, prisons, institutions, hospitals, anesthesia

Sample Dream Journal

Date: _____

Your Dream Program:

_____
_____
_____
_____
_____
_____
_____
_____
_____

Notes from Your Dream:

_____
_____
_____
_____

Your Interpretation:

Date: _____

Your Dream Program:

_____
_____
_____
_____
_____
_____
_____
_____
_____

Notes from Your Dream:

_____
_____
_____
_____
_____

Your Interpretation:

Date: _____

Your Dream Program:

_____
_____
_____
_____
_____
_____
_____
_____
_____

Notes from Your Dream:

_____
_____
_____
_____
_____

Your Interpretation:

Date: _____

Your Dream Program:

_____
_____
_____
_____
_____
_____
_____
_____
_____

Notes from Your Dream:

_____
_____
_____
_____
_____

Your Interpretation:

Date: _____

Your Dream Program:

_____
_____
_____
_____
_____
_____
_____
_____
_____

Notes from Your Dream:

_____
_____
_____
_____
_____

Your Interpretation:

Date: _____

Your Dream Program:

_____

_____

_____

_____

_____

_____

_____

_____

_____

Notes from Your Dream:

_____

_____

_____

_____

_____

Your Interpretation:

Made in the USA
Monee, IL
11 December 2022